The Ultim Customer Experience

*Five Steps to
Engage Your Colleagues,
Excite Your Customers, and
Enjoy Your Work!*

by

Scott McKain

Author of
"Create Distinction,"
"What Customers REALLY Want," &
"ALL Business is Show Business!"

© 2013; Scott McKain

Other books by Scott McKain:

"Create Distinction: What to Do When 'Great' Isn't Good Enough to Grow Your Business"

"Collapse of Distinction: Stand Out and Move Up While Your Competition Fails"

"What Customers REALLY Want"

"ALL Business is Show Business"

"Just Say YES: A Step Up to Success!" (with Antonia Barnes Boyle)

Dedication

Create Ultimate Customer Experiences!

The only purpose of this book is to assist you in delivering Ultimate Customer Experiences to YOUR customers and colleagues!

And, please know we stand ready to assist you in your efforts. From in-depth, on-going educational programs delivered online and in-person, to keynote speeches, to content-rich seminars, we have a myriad of formats ready to customize for your organization to assist you in delivering Ultimate Customer Experiences!

Contact your favorite speakers bureau, or:
Shelley Erwin
McKain Performance Group, Inc.
3095 Paseo Mountain Avenue
Henderson, NV 89052
800-838-6980
http://ScottMcKain.com

Table of Contents

Foreward

Almost every Sunday when I was a kid, my parents, sister, and myself would hop in our Chevy station wagon and make the drive of a few miles to get together with the families of either my Uncle Max or Uncle Jack.

My Dad, you see, was from a family of twelve kids – nine boys, three girls. They all shared a lot of experiences – from growing up dirt poor, to ten of the twelve serving in the armed forces and seeing action in either World War II or Korea. (As far as we know, that remains a record in our home state of Indiana for one group of brothers and sisters.)

Max and Jack were my Dad's favorites. Jack was older – and was the one who took my father under his wing. Max was younger, and Dad served the same role for him, even as they served together in Korea.

But, Jack and Max had an even more special bond, despite their age difference. They both were linemen. Max worked for what was then called Public Service Indiana – the investor-owned electric utility that's now Duke Energy. Jack was employed by the local rural electric cooperative.

As brothers often do when they start telling stories, each tried to top the other with how hard they worked, and how tough the conditions were. My Dad – a meat cutter and grocery store owner – always told the tale in the winter months of how difficult it was to butcher a cow for a farmer, working in a snowdrift on a windy night.

Jack and Max would laugh, and say that was nothing compared to being on an icy pole, working with electricity, on that same snowy, breezy evening.

But, there was another point that always stuck with me. Dad would tell them that the farmers would always mention how much they appreciated him coming out to the farm and helping them. At that point, Jack would always shake his head and say, "No one ever calls the electric company and tells them 'thanks' because their lights are on. But, let the ice take down a line, or a car wreck snap a pole, and EVERYONE calls to let us know what we're doing wrong."

It's true, even to this day isn't it?

You've done such a fantastic job, that people just assume that the service of Westar is always going to be there. Even your website says, "Every day, nearly 700,000 residential, commercial and industrial customers take us for granted. We wouldn't have it any other way."

However, that makes it easy for *you* to take your customers – *and the people you work with at Westar* -- for granted, as well.

> **Which, unfortunately, is the foundation of the very aspects and attitudes that can negatively impact and damage our safety.**

As you'll read in this book, there are TWO types of customers. One type is the external kind; those 700,000 or so that you traditionally think of…those Kansans who depend upon you to keep the lights on, and who make a monthly payment to make it so.

However, the second kind of customer is the INTERNAL kind -- those approximately 2,400 people you work with who depend upon you to do your job, so they can do theirs.

The attitude of "taking it for granted" may, unfortunately sometimes mean that you don't value the contribution of your colleagues as much as you should...

- ...or, that you've done something a gazillion times, so you don't even think about safety...

- ...or, that someone you work with won't put you in danger...

- ...or, that "customer service" means taking care of those outside Westar who write you checks for power -- when it should ALSO mean that you're looking out for each and every member of the internal team...

That's why you've been provided a book about customer service – even though your job may never put you face-to-face with any of those external customers who depend upon you to keep those 35,000 miles of transmission and distribution lines working -- and all of the other aspects required to serve them as they should be served.

It's critical that you know the importance of the INTERNAL customer...and that together at Westar, you work to keep each other safe – just as I wanted those who worked with my Uncle Jack and Uncle Max to make certain they got home to their families each night.

It's the reason for the "Ultimate Customer Experience ®" – a book that I truly hope you'll enjoy, and will be of value in everything you do.

Scott McKain

Introduction

Traveling to Jacksonville...

Middle seat, middle of the night.

On one side of me is a guy I am guessing is the latest parolee from my home state's reformatory. Squeezed into the aisle seat in my row must be a sumo-wrestling champion. Sandwiched between these two strangers, I'm doing my best at faking sleep, reading for a bit, sipping a Diet Coke, and fighting claustrophobia.

My fellow passengers seem tired and cranky, and so do the flight attendants. Even when the crew can summon the energy to muster a small semblance of a smile, their eyes are simultaneously sending subversive signals.

"Shark eyes, man, *shark eyes*..." the guy on the window says to me.

"Uh...what? I'm sorry," I reply, thinking I've missed something, "what did you say?"

"Look at 'er," he orders. "She's cold, man. She has shark eyes. Don't want to cross her -- she'd probably throw you off this thing."

"In mid-air!" Mr. Sumo inserts into the conversation -- then laughs heartily at his own attempt at humor. "She wouldn't give you a drink -- or a parachute -- on the way out, either!" He guffaws again at his own jokes.

How much longer is it to my destination?

I'm occupying space between these two because I'm heading to the northern Florida city of Jacksonville to make a presentation to a group of Merrill Lynch executives on the importance of great customer service. However, at this moment, I am certainly not on the receiving end of the type of experience I am strongly recommending every organization deliver to its clients!

And, while it would not be polite of me to reveal the name of the airline upon which I'm traveling at this point, they are known for "Delays Every Landing Through Atlanta!"

(On more than one occasion, they've also stood for: "Don't Expect Luggage To Arrive" -- and how about, "Didn't Even Leave The Airport!" However, as I am a Medallion Flyer with them, I won't complain too excessively!)

We're a couple of hours late, meaning I won't arrive in Jacksonville until a few minutes after midnight, and I'm booked for an early morning breakfast prior to my speech the following day. I'm already counting the few hours I will be able to sleep, knowing I have to be at my very best tomorrow for the audience.

It's easy to tell this is just another segment in a long day of flights for the crew. Get the cattle...uh, *passengers*...on the plane, shovel a drink and peanuts their way, hope they keep their mouths shut until landing, get them off the plane, then repeat the process. However, as we are undoubtedly riding upon their last flight of the day, as soon as they can get rid of us, their work is done. And, it seems from their demeanor, it cannot happen a moment too soon.

Mr. Sumo evidently swallows a peanut incorrectly and starts to cough. Between hacks, he smiles at the parolee and me and says,

"I'm OK...just a little too much salt!" Thankful I would not have to attempt to perform the Heimlich Maneuver on this man-mountain, I watched as he pressed the "Flight Attendant Call" button.

Slowly approaching the passenger, she stared at him coldly as he asked for a cup of water to relieve his coughing. Acting like a small child, she rolled her eyes to the ceiling, exhaled loudly, and said with a tone of disgust, "Certainly, sir. Just a moment."

About five minutes later, she approached with a cup of water, thrust it in Mr. Sumo's direction, and was gone before he could say, "Thank you."

After what seemed to be an eternity, the Captain announced we were beginning our *initial* descent into Jacksonville. (I have always wondered about the terms "*initial* descent" and "*final* approach." How many attempts does this pilot really need to get the plane on the ground, anyway?) Since I had been pinned into this middle seat for over an hour, I was hoping my legs would have the blood-flow necessary to stand up when we "reached our final destination."

The flight finally made the runway, the aircraft taxied to the assigned gate, and it was time for me to grab my beat-up carry-on, gather up my tired, old body, and head for the terminal.

Exiting the building, I realize passengers have formed a line for taxis -- meaning after my long flight, I am now going to have a substantial wait to get a ride to the hotel, which is not a pleasant development. I take my place at the end of the line.

Finally, after watching those in front of me get into other taxis whisking them to their various destinations, I have arrived at the front of the line. The NEXT cab is *MINE*!

Standing there, exhausted and half-asleep, I notice out of the corner of my eye that my cab is approaching. The driver halts his vehicle in front of me...and then...much to my surprise...jumps out of his cab, points his index finger in my direction and practically shouts at me:

"Are YOU ready for the BEST cab ride of your LIFE?"

Sheepishly, I look over each shoulder to see if he's speaking to someone else. When I realize the comment was directed at me, I shrug and say, "Uh...well...um...yeah. I guess so?"

He breaks into a broad smile and says, **"Well -- HOP ON IN!"**

Simultaneously, he jogs over to me, grabs my suitcase and pops open the trunk of his cab, as I climb into the back seat. He closes the trunk lid, jumps into the driver's seat, spins around toward me in the back, thrusts out his hand and inquires, "Mr. McKain?"

Stunned, I respond, "Yes -- but, HOW did you know my NAME?"

Again, he smiles. "Saw it on the name tag on your suitcase. Thought I might as well USE IT!"

Wiggling his hand a bit to reinforce he's waiting on a handshake, he states, ***"I'm TAXI TERRY!"***

In my fatigue, all I can think to myself is, "Great. I'm stuck with the motivational cab driver."

"Where we heading tonight, Mr. McKain?" he asks.

"The Marriott downtown," I reply.

"Great!" he exclaims, "Let's check out the weather!"

Weather? It hasn't even crossed my mind at midnight about what tomorrow's weather is going to be...when Taxi Terry touches the dashboard of his cab, and it seems to light up!

Embedded in the dash in a very elaborate bracket is an old PDA -- a Pocket PC -- with a magnifying glass over the screen, meaning I can clearly read it from the back seat. He has it directed to Weather.com for Jacksonville -- and I can clearly see the seconds ticking off -- meaning I now have the "up to the minute" weather forecast for my visit!

"I hope you play golf, Mr. McKain," he says, "because you are going to have a beautiful stay in Jacksonville!"

"Tell me, sir," he continues, "if you don't mind my asking, why are you here?"

"I'm in town to give a speech at the hotel to a group of professionals about customer service," I respond.

"Customer service!" he exclaims. **"I am SO *INTO* that!"**

I think, "No kidding. It shows." Then, he confounds my expectations once again.

He asks, "Would you mind if I record our conversation?" He starts reaching up toward his sun visor.

Meanwhile, I am thinking, "Who *IS* this guy?"

I have to ask the question, "Wait a second," I say. "Why are you so equipped to record the conversations that take place in your cab?"

"Well, you see, Mr. McKain," he responds slowly, "let's say Dr. Smith -- he's a local customer -- gets into my cab for a ride to the airport. And, during our conversation, he mentions that his daughter, Jill, has just enrolled at Vanderbilt University. As soon as he exits the cab, I hit the button and record that information."

Taxi Terry isn't done yet, however! "Every night when I return home, I take the information from these recordings I have made, and enter it into my database."

I'm thinking, "A CAB DRIVER...with a DATABASE?" By this point, I knew I was with someone really special!

"Then," Terry continued, "the next time that Dr. Smith makes a reservation, this information pops up on my computer. So, the Doctor gets into the cab, and I ask him, 'By the way, sir, how is Jill doing at Vanderbilt?'"

He smiles and says, "After that, do you think he will ever ride with anyone else?"

In the darkened back seat of a cab in Jacksonville, Florida, I shake my head and think to myself, "No. That doctor will never call *anyone else* for a trip to the airport!"

During our ride, Taxi Terry educates me on some of his other approaches to the customer experience -- but he still has another surprise for me!

In just about every "normal" cab ride I have experienced on a business trip, upon arrival at the destination, the driver presents the passenger with two forms -- sometimes printed on opposite sides of the same card, occasionally on separate papers -- one is a receipt, so the rider can file for expense reimbursement or a tax deduction; and, the second is a business card, in hopes the passenger will request the same driver for a return trip once your meeting is near its conclusion.

On this extraordinary trip, however, Taxi Terry pulled in front of the hotel, ran to the trunk of his car, removed my bag and held it as if were a family member. He gently handed the bag to a waiting bellman and said he was "Delivering Mr. McKain and his bag!"

Then, he turns to me without a card or paper or form in his hand and says, "Mr. McKain, I realize you are going to need a receipt to document the trip for your business purposes. AND, someone brought you here -- so someone is going to have to take you back to the airport -- and, I hope that's ME!"

He continued, "You can print your receipt and schedule your return trip on my website" -- and I'm thinking, "A cab driver...with a WEBSITE?" -- "at," he continued, "www.TaxiTerry.com!"

However, he still was not finished! "One more thing, Mr. McKain?" he requested. "You mentioned you fly a great deal...which probably means you are riding in a lot of cabs. Well," he continued, "I'm franchising these ideas! So, if you ever run into a cab driver who could use some help with customer service," (and I am thinking that would probably be ALL OF THEM!) "then you just tell them about *TAXI TERRY!"*

I wanted to give him a standing ovation on the spot! It was a perfect example of an **Ultimate Customer Experience!**

We will continue to refer to Taxi Terry's excellence throughout this book -- however, start now to consider this question: What steps did Taxi Terry take that the flight attendants on my flight did NOT?

The Ultimate Customer Experience

Stop and consider for a moment a time when YOU were a customer and treated in a manner that you would emphatically declare to be an "ultimate experience."

Write down what it was -- specifically -- regarding the way you interacted with a customer representative, clerk, sales person, or member of a support team that made this particular situation stand out as being an "ultimate experience."

Maybe it was a terrific product that made your heart sing…service that made you feel like you were a highly valued client...a specific compliment from a sales associate...perhaps a movie that made you laugh or cry -- or both! What was the last time when you were a customer and you felt YOU received an "Ultimate Customer Experience?"

Seriously. Stop right now…and write it down!

We will refer again throughout the book to this experience you have noted!

To begin, let's expand our vision of what a "customer" truly is. Dictionary.com states that the definition of a customer is "a person of a specified kind that one has to deal with."

*Since people of a "specified kind" that YOU "have to deal with" include the colleagues that you work with, we are going to call them **"internal customers"** – and the people who spend money for the products and services of your company are called **"external customers."***

*When you see just the term "customer," it means that the principles we are discussing can be applied to **either or both** internal and external people whom you have to consider. You'll see more on this important concept in just a moment...now let's examine YOUR "Ultimate Customer Experience" with these two critical points:*

1) The experience was obviously powerful.

I'll bet you've been a customer in literally thousands of situations at a wide variety of businesses. From the store where you buy groceries, to the shop where you get your car serviced...from the hotel where you stayed on vacation, to the restaurant where you had dinner last weekend – your experience as a customer is both deep (going repeatedly to the same places) and wide (doing business at a large number of establishments).

In other words, when it comes to BEING a customer...*you are an expert!*

Notice, as well, that out of your literally thousands of experiences you have had as a customer, the ones that first came to mind -- and the single one you selected to write down -- was obviously more powerful and compelling than the rest. (It's why you thought of it as the answer to the question!)

Therefore, it is logical to assume you are not only an expert --
you also can determine what is an Ultimate Customer Experience
is to *you*! Doesn't it make sense that if you can determine what
creates a UCE for you, those same aspects will assist you in
creating Ultimate Customer Experiences for others?

The ride with Taxi Terry was obviously an incredibly powerful
experience for me -- it's why I not only remember it, it is why I've
written here about it, and why a video of me telling this story has
been posted on YouTube and viewed (at the time I'm writing this)
over 90,000 times by people all over the world! Ultimate
Customer Experiences create a powerful impact upon their
recipients -- and more!

We will leverage the experience you have as a customer to assist
you in creating the "Ultimate Customer Experience" for your
customers – internal and external!

**2) WHY would ANY customer CHOOSE to receive *less* than
you did in the instance you have just recalled?**

Wouldn't YOU like to be treated *ALL of the time* in the superior
manner you've just recalled? If you entered a cab for a ride,
wouldn't you desire a driver like Taxi Terry? Of course! *We ALL
would!*

So…if you would like to experience a UCE when you do
business…why wouldn't you want to create the very same
amazing connection with **your** customers?

Here's part of what I've learned from over two decades of
studying the importance of the customer experience:

We fail to create the very experiences we desire to receive, because when we go to work, we think like an employee...NOT like a **CUSTOMER***!*

Consider this point: There are very few "help" conferences...there are LOTS of "*sales*" conferences! We seldom assemble our team and really focus upon how we can be of greater assistance to our customers. Yet, we constantly have meetings on how we can sell more of our products and services to customers and prospects.

Few organizations will seek outside expertise to assist them in connecting more emotionally with their clients – yet, many will hire "efficiency experts" to assist them in doing their jobs and delivering their products faster and cheaper.

We have meetings about everything under the sun when it comes to being more productive or ways to perform our tasks more efficiently. Yet, it is not very often that we talk about how we can serve our colleagues more effectively – or, let them know what they can do so that we can attain a higher level of performance.

Then, we wonder why customers aren't loyal and more engaged with us!

Both my research and my professional experience have taught me that both individuals and organizations willing to focus upon creating Ultimate Customer Experiences will discover -- because UCE's generate from customers the type of engagement that I have already displayed toward Taxi Terry – that not only are external customers better taken care of; you, and your colleagues, will find your work more enjoyable and productive!

The purpose of this book...and your choice to read it.

The reason for existence of this short book is to illuminate for you five fundamental aspects toward creating "Ultimate Customer Experiences" for the clients and prospects you deal with every single day.

If your company gave you this book...it says some very positive points about *them*!

First, it means they are committed to improving the experiences you create for customers and colleagues. *NO organization or individual would invest in an activity in which they had little interest!*

You wouldn't buy season tickets to the games of a sports team you didn't care about. You would never watch every episode of a television show you didn't enjoy! And, your company would not have given you this book if they weren't focused on your important role in enhancing the customer experience.

It also says they are interested in YOU! (Remember, you don't invest in something you aren't interested in!) Your company recognizes YOU are their most important asset!

What if you are investing the time to actually read this book?

Well, it obviously means you have initiative in taking the most important step any of us can ever take – *personal growth!* You don't acquire AND read a book if all you want to do is tread water and remain the same. You made this effort because you have made a decision to improve yourself, personally and professionally!

But, what if the people you work with do not have the same dedication to internal and external customers as you?

Honestly…that's a tough one. It's so much easier to create Ultimate Customer Experiences when the commitment runs throughout the organization. However – *and this is a very important point* – you have to take personal responsibility for how you engage the internal or external customers with whom you have contact!

Think about it! I've received great service from companies that I KNOW couldn't give a darn about my business. You have, too, I'll wager! How did that happen?

There is only one possible answer: An *individual* cared more about you than the obvious deficiencies in their colleague's approach to dealing with customers.

There will be times that you may question whether or not it is worth it to go the extra mile to serve customers, if you aren't receiving the support you deserve.

This can create enormous difficulties for customers. Too many people, as my friend, blogger Seth Simonds states, seem to be behaving as if the confirmation of their personal importance fails to come from above in the organization, they will *extract it* from below. A slang term used in the United States is "mall cop syndrome" -- it is meant to criticize those who people who use the authority of their position to hide behind "company policy" or "corporate procedures" to make things tougher on the very people they should be serving -- customers! In some cases, for some people, the top level doesn't make us feel important, so we take it out on our colleagues or our customers and show them that we are the gatekeepers, totally in charge of their customer experience.

You are better than that.

That's why you're reading this book…and why you are making the commitment to create and deliver the **Ultimate Customer Experience!**

I will let you in on a secret…there is nothing in this book new or exclusively original to me. No groundbreaking or revolutionary approaches, no business school theories or high-level management concepts for you to consider.

This is a book intended for ALL of us…from the management team to front line employees…from executives to executive assistants…to remind all of us of some basic steps we already know, but often fail to consistently execute. Steps that enable us to connect with the very people who determine our success and our future – customers!

Look, I realize that you may think of "customers" and only visualize those *outside* the organization purchasing our products and services.

However, what if you don't deal directly with external customers?

One of the most important concepts for you to integrate in your efforts is "internal customers." Popularized in the 1950's by Romanian-born management consultant, Dr. Joseph Juran, it still has great application today.

The Elsmar Cove Forum describes it this way: "A simple definition of an internal customer is anyone within an organization who at any time is dependent on anyone else within the organization."

It will assist you to develop categories, listing all of the internal customers you serve and their individual requirements and needs. In addition, make a list of those departments and individuals within your organization who are serving YOU – the places where you are the internal customer.

This is important, because it means if your boss fails to get you the information or training you need to do your job, he or she has failed YOU – the internal customer! Therefore, internal customers consist of *everyone* up AND down within the organization who would be impacted if you failed to do your job.

And, just as with external customers…internal customers seek, desire, and deserve an "Ultimate Customer Experience!"

As we discuss UCE's in this book, most of the examples will revolve around external customers. *However, if your role is exclusively serving internal ones, the steps to creating the Ultimate Customer Experience are practically identical.*

There are five simple steps to creating an Ultimate Customer Experience:

- *Make a GREAT Impression*
- *Don't Make It Right…GET It Right!*
- *Serve With Empathy*
- *Connect With Emotion*
- *Take Personal Responsibility*

However, one of the most interesting aspects about creating an ultimate customer experience is found in the fact that to do so...it doesn't begin with the "experience" at all.

Step One: Make a GREAT Impression

Part of the challenge we encounter in creating Ultimate Customer Experiences stems from the fact we have three terms that should have different definitions -- yet are traditionally used interchangeably. How many times have you heard these phrases?

- *Customer satisfaction*
- *Customer service*
- *Customer experience*

My bet is when you notice these terms being used, there is very little distinction made between them.

Until we understand these three are *very* dissimilar (especially when we examine them from the *customer's* point of view), it will be extraordinarily difficult to develop and execute the strategies necessary to create UCE's. In other words, if we cannot define what we are doing – how in the world can we accomplish it?

As we proceed, you will learn how these are fundamentally different aspects of our relationship with the customer. Later in this book, you will learn the three distinct levels upon which we interact with all of our customers.

However…let's begin at a pretty obvious place: *the beginning!* Consider this story:

Dining with my wife this past Valentine's Day, the waiter approached our table in the crowded restaurant. "I'm Jason, I'll be serving you tonight," he stated curtly. He was sweating profusely and scowling. "I'd better get your drink order now, because I'm really slammed. If you know what you want to eat, just go ahead and tell me that now, too." Wow. *That* really enhanced the romantic atmosphere I was hoping to create!

The problem for Jason and his restaurant is that no matter what happens next, the experience of the evening is soiled. We wanted to have a nice, romantic Valentine's Day dinner, but instead our first impression is that it's going to be a challenging night with a difficult server.

Don't get me wrong. I'm sorry that Jason is "slammed" – but what did he expect on Valentine's evening? And, does he really think *his* problems should be transmitted to the people in charge of the table's post-meal tipping decision? **The problem is, he didn't stop to think about the importance and power of first impressions.**

As I am writing this, I am sitting on a United flight from Indianapolis to Denver, my shoes are shined, I'm wearing my best dark suit, my shirt is pressed and I'm sporting a stylish tie. I'm doing my best to create a professional and powerful image, because, when I arrive I will be creating something very powerful – *an impression.*

My mother back home in tiny Crothersville, Indiana isn't an expert when it comes to business, but neither the march of time nor technology has made one of her parental clichés outmoded: **"You never get a second chance to make a first impression."**

But, it is not just "first" impressions that count! *Every* time you communicate with an internal or external customer, you're making an impression. Just about every office I've visited, plant that I have been to, or team I have encountered, has that guy who is grumpy in the morning, or the gal who rolls her eyes whenever someone makes a statement. Each time they make that impression upon their internal customers, the respect and credibility they have is damaged just a bit.

However, if that's the case, why do many professionals fail to understand its impact?

For example, Human Resources executives tell me – and my personal experience supports – during the interview process, prospective employees often kill their chances by focusing their communication upon what *they want* from the job, rather than what they can *contribute to the organization* where they are applying for a position.

Certainly, part of that interviewing process has to contain details about your experience and education. However, what every organization seeks from you in an interview is for you to display a passion for performance directed toward the company from which you seek employment. (Who would want to hire a future internal customer who only cares about himself, or who only desires to advance herself and not the team?)

A website (GradView.com) lists some pretty awful approaches taken by some interviewees:

- *Applicant stretched out on the floor to fill out the job application.*
- *Applicant brought her large dog to the interview.*
- *Applicant chewed bubble gum and constantly blew bubbles.*
- *Applicant wore a Walkman, claiming she could listen to the interviewer and the music at the same time.*
- *Balding applicant abruptly excused himself and returned to the office a few minutes later, wearing a hairpiece.*
- *Applicant challenged the interviewer to arm wrestle.*
- *Applicant asked to see the interviewer's resume to see if the personnel executive was qualified to interview him.*
- *Applicant announced she hadn't had lunch and proceeded to eat a hamburger and french fries during the interview.*
- *Applicant wore a jogging suite to interview for the*

position of financial vice-president. (Yes, dress codes are getting more casual. But please.)

- *Applicant said if he were hired, he would demonstrate his loyalty by having the corporate logo tattooed on his forearm.*
- *Applicant interrupted to phone his therapist for advice on answering specific interview questions.*
- *Applicant refused to get out of his chair until interviewer agreed to hire him. Interviewer had to call the police to have him removed.*
- *Applicant said he wasn't interested because the job paid too much.*
- *A telephone call came in for the job applicant. His side of the conversation went as follows: "Which company? When do I start? What's the salary?" When the interviewer said he assumed the applicant was not interested in completing the interview, he promptly responded, "I am as long as you'll pay me more." The interviewer did not hire him, and later found out there was no other job offer--it was a scam to get a better offer.*
- *Applicant's attaché case opened when he picked it up and the contents spilled, revealing women's undergarments and assorted makeup and perfume.*
- *Applicant said he didn't really want to get a job, but the unemployment office needed proof he was looking for one.*

Funny, of course, but what does this have to do with customer experiences? Well, first, the most terrifying aspect is that these people are working *somewhere* – and, what type of customer experiences do you suppose they are creating for the internal and external customers they encounter?

(And, by the way, you may want to share this information with any young family members or other friends who will be interviewing as they head out into the job market! It can make the difference between whether they receive an employment opportunity...*or not.*)

More importantly, however, is the lack of knowledge about how to create a positive professional impression. And, let's face it, the impressions we create in our professional life follow the same model as in our personal one.

How do you create a positive impression? Center your thinking on these three points:

1. ***Everything matters***
2. ***Focus on the other***
3. ***Be your best self***

First, everything matters. The more important the impression, the greater your focus should be on everything.

Legend has it that Henry Ford was interviewing a prospective executive over breakfast for a major management position with his then-rapidly growing company. When the candidate took the shaker and salted eggs he had yet to taste, the cantankerous Ford said, "This interview is over."

When asked to explain by the stunned executive, Ford replied, "If you'll salt eggs you have yet to taste without knowing whether or not they need it, you'll spend my money without knowing whether or not it will bring results."

Thankfully, not every customer is as persnickety as Ford was as an interviewer. However, for all of us evaluating an impression, *everything* – no matter how small – *matters*.

Second, focus on the other – as in the *other person*; from the internal customer to the blind date across the table.

If you center your communication upon yourself, you run the risk of appearing vain, arrogant or insecure. If you channel your strengths to impact their needs, wants and concerns, you appear confident and the kind of person we all want as a colleague or customer.

Third, be your *best* self. Usually, this is the point where someone says that you should just "be yourself." However, that's not what makes the best impression.

"Being myself" *could* include the self that smokes too many cigars at a local steakhouse or gets too rowdy at football games. My "best self" is the one who is attuned to the challenges and needs of others, who seeks to identify solutions rather than problems and who projects strength through humility. I would suggest that is your "best self" too.

One of my favorite websites, AllBusiness.com, recently had a post quoting an article by Barry Himmel, originally published in "Rental Product News," regarding the impact of first impressions on a customer.

"Consider these two phone interactions," the article asks.

"Example 1:

- *Inside sales coordinator: "ABC Rentals, how can I help you?"*
- *Customer: "I need to rent a backhoe for a week."*
- *Inside sales coordinator: "OK, what size backhoe?"*
- Example 2
- *Inside sales coordinator: "Thank you for calling ABC Rentals, this is Barry. How can I help you?"*
- *Customer: "I need to rent a backhoe for a week."*
- *Inside sales coordinator: "Great, I will be happy to help you with that. May I get your name please?"*

As Himmel states in the article, "The differences might seem slight, but are actually significant. The personalization in the second example takes almost no additional time, but it can leave a significant impact on your customer."

Remember my encounter with Taxi Terry? The impression he created was *incredible*!

First, he set the stage for an ultimate customer experience – "Are you ready for the BEST cab ride of your life?" he asked. If we were to survey your customers about the experience they anticipated based upon the impression they had of you – what would their answers be? Are you Taxi Terry? Or the grumpy guy or eye-rolling gal we mentioned earlier?

(By the way, to be clear, these are just examples...*nothing more!* There are plenty of grumpy gals and eye-rolling guys – it's NOT meant to be gender specific. It's just meant to point out that there are some people who – either through ignorance or choice – don't create impressions that contribute to a positive experience for their colleagues and customers.)

Second, Taxi Terry learned my name – then used it repeatedly in the conversation. There was no doubt in my mind he had made an effort to connect with me personally, and – as Barry Himmel suggests in the previously mentioned article – his personalization made a significant impact upon this customer!

Had Taxi Terry had a bad day on the particular date I was riding in his cab? Honestly...I don't know! He made the trip all about *my* needs and wants, not his! Unlike Jason, the waiter from the earlier example, Terry put his effort and focus upon "the other" – *the customer* – instead of upon himself.

My friend and famed motivational speaker, the late Zig Ziglar, is often quoted as saying, "You can have everything in life that you want -- if you just give enough other people what *they* want."

Jason the waiter wasn't too concerned about what we wanted. He was "slammed" and preferred to get our ordering...and dining...over with as quickly as possible to serve his need to turn the table and make more money. We never returned to that restaurant again, because of the terrible experience – for which the tone was firmly set by the first impression.

On the other hand, every time I go to Jacksonville, Florida, Taxi Terry is there to pick me up! I've done business multiple times with Terry – and I know of many other people who have used his services based upon my recommendations.

The point is, by creating Ultimate Customer Experiences – beginning with an extraordinary impression – Terry is achieving the high volume of business he desires. He is "getting what he wants" by giving his customers "what they want!"

However, as another great motivational speaker – the late Jim Rohn – used to say, "That which is easy to do is also easy NOT to do. Which explains why most people won't do it!"

In other words, it's easy to answer the phone in the manner of the previous "Example Two." It is so easy, in fact, most people will just settle for doing it like "Example One." It's almost TOO simple! It doesn't require the expenditure of any funds – and only costs you a tiny bit of effort and discipline – yet, it makes such an extraordinary difference!

How many cab drivers *could* have said, "Are you ready for the BEST cab ride of your life?" The answer, of course: ALL OF THEM!

Yet, up until my encounter with Taxi Terry, how many had said that to me? The answer, of course: NONE OF THEM!

Naturally, YOU can do BETTER! And the way you begin to create Ultimate Customer Experiences is to start with an "ultimate first impression."

UCE Checklist

1. Remember, ***"Everything matters."*** Take an objective look at the impression you are creating – everything from your appearance and presentation, to the words you say and how they are said.
   a. What can you do to make everything absolutely perfect?
2. What can you say – and *do* – to PROVE to internal and external customers that your focus is upon them, and not upon yourself?
   a. Write it out – and practice it!
3. How would you define your "best self"? What would your "best self" say to a customer or prospect? (Especially one with a question or problem, by the way.) Remember, one way to determine this is simply to recollect how YOU like to be treated.
   a. How much enthusiasm would your "best self" display?
4. It doesn't take much – but the effort you make in personalizing your communication has a significant impact upon prospects and customers!
   a. Develop three specific ways you can personalize the communication you have with customers to a greater extent.
5. Outline two additional and specific approaches you can implement to make a more positive and compelling impression!

Step Two: Don't Make It Right...GET It Right!

One of the most important points anyone could ever make about the customer experience with you and your organization is simply this:

Your customer does not want you to "MAKE" it right!

Your customer wants you to "GET" it right!

In other words, putting a smile on your face and knowing the customer's name will make a great impression – and, as we've already learned, that is vital. However, it is not nearly enough to achieve an Ultimate Customer Experience. If the product doesn't work, if my lights go off, if the food is awful at the restaurant, if the rental car breaks down, if the service doesn't live up to expectations – if something is wrong, customers are (rightfully!) disappointed.

For any organization or professional to truly excel, they must understand that each of these levels of interaction as unique – and develop a specific plan to strategically improve performance at each level.

The three levels of customer interaction are:

Level One: Processing – the basic elements of the transaction; the aspects of any situation the customer has a right to expect you to deliver upon -- since they have chosen to spend money with, or be employed with, *you* and your organization.

Level Two: Service – the steps you will undertake to make Processing more efficient, palatable, enjoyable, or friendly to your customer to enhance the likelihood they will repeat their experience.

Level Three: Experience – the commitment of the individual and the organization for a connectivity to ensure your interactions with customers are intensely personal and include an element of emotion. It is only at *this* point loyalty from the client toward your organization (or you) is generated.

It is also essential to note these three levels are **progressive**. In other words, if a customer's needs are not met at the lower level, activities at higher levels are irrelevant to sustaining loyalty. We will examine this point in more detail a little later.

Let's begin where we should – at the first level: **Processing**.

Note, however, that mere "Processing" means that you perfectly execute what the customer has a right to expect. (It should go without saying that internal customers have a right to expect you to do your job – and external customers have a right to expect that they will receive their "money's worth" when they do business with you and your organization.) It means everything is done properly. It means you "*get* it right" for your customer!

It's important to remember, however, our goal is to create "Ultimate Customer Experiences" – so just giving the customer merely what they have a reasonable right to expect does not fulfill our total objective. It is, however, an important and vital early step.

In fact, many studies suggest customers do not have expectations of us that are positive. Many of our prospects and customers expect the worst – merely hoping for the best. So, do you believe that "meeting customer expectations" – to use that old business cliché – is nearly good enough? Of course not!

Why do customers feel that way? (Perhaps, instead, the question should be phrased: "Why do you and I feel that way when WE are the customers?") I would suggest it is because of these kinds of common experiences:

Example One:

You have probably been there a million times -- you're fourth in line as you are driving through a local fast food restaurant. The line of cars moves slowly as they make their way through the line to arrive at the menu board, where customers can place an order.

As you finally make it to the point where you can order your lunch, you are greeted with this sound from the speaker: "GOODAFTERNOONWELCOMETOBURGERKINGMAYITA KEYOURORDERPLEASE?"

The over-modulation from the speaker causes you to briefly recall a rock concert you attended in the early '70's. (Why does it seem that technology has advanced everything except the speakers at drive-thrus?) You place your order for lunch and then hear: "THANKYOUNEXTWINDOW"

A disinterested, bored cashier takes your money and points you to the next window, where a disinterested clerk pitches a bag of food at you. Have a nice lunch.

Sound familiar? Here's another:

Example Two:

You're waiting in a long line at the airport. When you finally arrive at the front, a ticket agent shouts, "NEXT!" You walk up, to be greeted with these words: "Where's your destination today?" When you answer his question, he then responds with the ever personal, "Name?"

He types your name and some mysterious code into the computer. He scrunches his mouth and waits, never looking at you. Evidently the computer screen has told the agent that you do, in fact, have a reservation – even an e-ticket for the flight – so the agent responds to his new information by saying, "Checking bags today?"

You check your bag, get your boarding pass, show your ID – and the agent never uses your name in the conversation.

Now it's time for the exhilarating segment of the trip we call "airport security." You stand in a long queue to get to the point of screening – a line so enormous that it is putting you in danger of missing your plane. When you arrive at the front, you're told to strip off your belt, shoes and dignity. You remove your laptop from your briefcase, spilling several items that you had carefully packed along the way. Thankfully, you didn't "beep" – and you can now make the mad dash so you won't miss your flight.

You arrive at the gate and the boarding process is like cattle at a slaughterhouse. The gate agent allows those with "special needs," children, elite-level fliers, passengers in first class and those wearing yellow with a middle name of "Sue" to board ahead of you. Then the people in the rear, then the middle and by the time your group is announced you are thankful that you have no carry-on to attempt to place in the already-full overhead compartments.

You finally take your seat – one row ahead of the mother traveling with a crying baby and a four year old who won't stop kicking your seat. The frazzled flight attendants, who must serve a full plane in a short haul, thrust a lukewarm cup of coffee your way. After sixty minutes trapped in hell, you finally land at your destination.

They believe they did their job!

In both of these cases, the business where you were a customer would – perhaps rightly – tell you that they "did their job." You were delivered a meal…you were delivered to your destination. You got your food and you didn't have to wait an inordinate amount of time. You got where you wanted to go, had a cup of coffee and arrived approximately on time.

The problem is that there is a bad taste in your mouth.

You were *processed* -- Level One – but it just isn't enough in today's marketplace. The problem is, many organizations and professionals confuse processing with service – in turn, creating a significant portion of the problems customers have with the level of customer service they're receiving.

In other words, because customers and companies define the very nature of customer service differently, many organizations miss the mark and fail to understand why.

Please don't misunderstand me – it is vital to improve the way in which your organization executes the way you process your customer's transactions! **To take it to the "next" level, you first have to get it right at this one.** It is an absolute "must" to get it right for the people who choose to invest their time and money with you and your organization.

The suggestion here is that every organization would be much better off if every professional working there would take just a moment to ask two simple questions when it comes to "getting it right":

    1. How can I improve the product or service we sell, so customers receive more than they expect?

2. *How can I deliver our product or service to our customers so the transaction doesn't seem to "mechanical"?*

Improving "Getting it Right"

In it's simplest form, improvement is achieved every time you ask yourself, "How can I do my job better?" There is no better example than the one cited by my long-time close friend, Mark Sanborn, in his bestselling book, "The Fred Factor." (Broadway Business; 2004)

In this terrific work, Mark reveals the true story of the remarkable man who delivered his mail every day – Fred the Postman. Fred took great pride in loving his job and genuinely caring about the people he served. In the book, Fred is constantly going the extra mile handling the mail - and sometimes watching over the houses - of the people on his route, treating everyone he meets as a friend. Where others might see delivering mail as monotonous drudgery, Fred sees an opportunity to make a difference in the lives of those he serves.

I've always loved Mark's subtitle for the book: "How Passion in Your Work and Life Can Turn the Ordinary into the Extraordinary." In other words, no one can have more impact on "getting it right" than you! (Remember the old line about a "chain is only as strong as its weakest link"? If you are stronger and better, so is the entire organizational chain.) Mark Sanborn's book also proves that EVERYONE – no matter where you work, or what you do – can deliver an Ultimate Customer Experience to internal and external customers.

Taxi Terry could have said to himself, "Hey – I got the guy from the airport to the hotel. I delivered him to exactly the right spot he requested. I got it right!" However, there is no doubt it wasn't enough for Terry to do the bare minimum. I'm certain he asked himself, "What MORE can I do to truly 'get it right?'"

By asking – even to the point of *demanding* – more of yourself, you begin the process that moves you to a higher level than perhaps even you've imagined!

If you can do your job in the amazing way that Fred the Postman – or Taxi Terry – do theirs, maybe someday, someone will write a book about YOU!

But, what if we don't "get it right"?

We are all human – which means that no matter what we do, no matter where in the world we work, no matter what organization we are going to work for – we are going to make mistakes.

If customers want us to "get it right" – and we fail – then what?

Then…*and ONLY then*…customers want you to "**make** it right."

Customers want to know you have done everything humanly possible to deal with them at Level One. They crave a reason to believe you have gone "above and beyond" to provide them with what they have a reasonable right to expect, because they have chosen to do business with you.

However – and this may come as a surprise to some – believe it or not, customers are people, too! Just as you, customers have made mistakes where they work and live, and therefore, can be understanding when it fails to go exactly as you would prefer.

My bet is your experience is similar to mine – when customers believe you have done everything humanly possible to uphold your part of the deal, they are forgiving when it isn't exactly right.

Working out of my home, I was awaiting an important delivery prior to a significant conference call, and, unfortunately, the delivery service was late. This morning was in the midst of a strong spring thunderstorm; however, my previous experience led me to believe in their promptness, regardless of the situation.

I called their toll-free number, used the tracking code, and let them know their delivery was twenty minutes late! I learned the truck was near – however, they were uncertain at the moment why it was running past the contracted delivery time.

The operator told me she would promptly call me back with the information. A few minutes later, as promised, I received a call. "Unfortunately, your driver has had a flat tire," the operator said. "He will be at your door in the next ten minutes." About three minutes later, my doorbell rang.

There stood a soaking wet delivery employee, with hands dirty from changing a tire. He had a plastic wrap to protect my package – even as he was being soaked from the storm. "I am so sorry to be late, sir!" he told me. "What can we do to make this right for you?"

I asked, "What happened?"

"In the rain, a pothole filled with water, and I didn't see it. When I hit it, it blew out my tire – so, to make it here, I had to change the tire as quickly as I could. I'm sorry it made me late!"

My attitude has just performed a complete reversal! He has gone from an incompetent driver, twenty minutes late…to a HERO who braved the elements, changed a tire in the rain, found my house and delivered my package – and was ONLY twenty minutes behind schedule!

I told him there was nothing on earth needed to make it better, I was a satisfied customer – and, offered him a hot cup of coffee and a towel!

However, consider this: What would my attitude have been if, instead, he said, "Dude! You ever drive when it's raining like this? This is no fun, man. You should be happy I'm only twenty or so minutes late. I busted my tail to get your package here. Cut me some slack – give me a break!"

How many times has that attitude been inflicted upon you when YOU are the customer? The waiter blames the slow meal on the kitchen; the manufacturer blames the late delivery on their suppliers; the speaker blames the audience; the manager blames the employees; the employees blame the…well, you get the idea. At many organizations, no one wants to take personal responsibility – and the customer always seems to be the one who ends up as loser.

If you have experienced this – it probably means that *your* customers have, too! And, it drives us all crazy! (Which explains the reason customers do not prefer you to "make" it right as a first response!)

The next step…

Congratulations! You "got it right" for your customer! It is an important milestone on the journey to create an Ultimate Customer Experience.

However, customers do not want to perceive doing business with you is overly mechanical or systematic. It's an ironic aspect of dealing with people – we want you to have the systems in place to deliver perfect processing. Yet, at the same time, we do not want to FEEL as if we are merely a number being processed!

It means the next step is making customers feel more engaged in the interactions we have with them. It's discovered in the delivery of true customer *service*!

UCE Checklist

1. What does "getting it right" mean to YOUR customers?
    a. How do you know?
        i. Research
        ii. Experience
        iii. Asking them in person?
    b. List three ways you can improve "getting it right" for your customers
2. There are three levels of customer interaction
    a. Processing; Service; Experience
    b. "Getting it right" primarily involves Level One: Processing
3. Customers want to be processed perfectly – and enthusiastically
    a. "The Fred Factor" is an excellent example of how passion makes work – and customers – more productive
    b. How do you bring passion to your work and life?
    c. List three steps you take to make work more compelling
4. Customers only accept "making" it right when they know you've done everything possible to "get" it right!
    a. Name two occasions you have had to "make it right."
    b. How did customers respond?
    c. How could it have been handled more productively?

Step Three: Serve With Empathy

Sure, you've heard the old line, "Service with a smile!" Would that really be what the customer is seeking if you are running a funeral home?

How about an automobile body shop, and you have just had your dream car towed in after an accident? It seems a wide-tooth, insincere grin would make you want to slap the person behind the counter, not give them your business.

Let's break this short step down, based upon its three important words:

"**Serve**" – the customer – whether an internal one where you work, or an external one, coming and spending money with you -- desires you to assist them. Unless you are clearly labeled as a "self-service" establishment, your customer also expects you to be of assistance to them. (And, even if you ARE "self-serve," the customer usually encounters a cashier, or some other employee, in the process. Which, of course, means their evaluation of the business will be based, in part, on the attitude the employee displays toward the customer – even though the customer has "served" herself!)

"**With**" – means service alone isn't enough. To answer the phone on the first ring, ensuring the customer doesn't have to wait, is good service. However, it is not enough to fulfill the customer's expectations. There is something required to be associated *with* service in order to move us toward the standard of "ultimate" we desire.

"**Empathy**" – is defined by Dictionary.com as "the intellectual identification with or vicarious experiencing of the feelings, thoughts, or attitudes of another." In other words, we connect with the customer in a manner that displays we can – and *do* -- relate to their feelings, thoughts, or attitudes.

Let's examine "Serve With Empathy" in greater detail.

"Serve"…

No matter what your organization does, "serving" a customer is at the core.

In February 2007, the Hesperia, California Star newspaper ran a story on the city's new mayor, Rita Vogler. The article cited her previous jobs -- which included being a "carhop" (a waitress at a drive-in restaurant, where the customers dine in their cars), a clerk in a grocery store, and owner of a very successful travel agency. The reporter, Peter Day, asked the newly elected mayor what all of these different – and highly diverse – jobs had in common with her new position as mayor?

"Customer service," Vogler emphatically answered, "and hoping that you make a difference in someone's life, with a smile."

She continued, "'I get to have wonderful clients that come in,' she said. 'I get to know about their families and their quality of life.'"

The article makes it obvious Vogler believes through her experiences in serving customers in many capacities, she will be better at leading her colleagues and serving the citizens who elected her mayor of their community. In other words, serving is a transferable skill. If you can excel at serving others in one situation, you have the ability to discover how you can serve them more effectively, no matter where you work or what you do.

Scott McKain

It begins with your attitude!

When you get right down to it, "serve" begins with your attitude. If you have an attitude of service…you are probably taking the first important steps to delivering an ultimate customer experience.

However, if you believe customers are those people who get in the way as you are trying to get your work done…chances are you aren't creating the types of compelling experiences your customers will want to repeat.

Bert Boeckmann started out at Galpin Motors as a salesman in 1953. He took over as company president in 1963, became the majority owner in 1964, and sole owner in 1968. Consider that – from salesman to being the *owner* of the business in just fifteen years! How did that happen?

Boeckmann told "Smart Business: Los Angeles" in 2007 that you can "never lose sight of the reason why you are in business" -- and he says it is not just to sell your product or service. It's to *take care of the people* who use your product or service.

"We have no reason to be here unless we serve our customers the way they deserve to be treated," he says. "A lot of people say, 'I don't want to be a servant,' but that's not what we're talking about."

Boeckmann continues, "We're here for a paycheck -- but if you're working *just* for a paycheck you might not be serving the customer the way you should. But if you are serving the customer the way you should, you'll definitely get a paycheck." (emphasis added)

So, what does "serving the customer" *really* mean?

It's easy to find a number of widely varied definitions. The website Financial Crisis 2009 asked its readers to weigh in with their ideas on its meaning. Here are a few:

- *Getting what I need as quickly and as simply as possible.*
- *The ability to present a competent solution to your customer at the same time showering your customer with assurance, convenience, sense of urgency, and esprit de corps.*
- *It is serving your client with care, attention, and most of all, giving customers satisfaction when it comes to handling inquiries or even complaints.*
- *Making sure both the customer and business benefit from each transaction. (As in, customer knows the product buys it leaves happy and doesn't return product)*
- *Treating the customers the way you expect to be treated when you go shopping. Then explain how you expect to be treated and how you strive to make each person's experience a positive one.*
- *Genuinely caring for customers.*
- *To me it means a caring, attentive individual who is dedicated to serving the customer's needs, and providing assistance whenever needed.*

As you can see, there are many definitions of customer service – this list barely scratches the surface! Why are there so many varied descriptions of something we all seek? Consider these two rationales:

First, we've lumped too many aspects of our interactions with customers into a "catch-all" term like "customer service." (Remember the Three Levels of Customer Interaction? We often make the mistake of bundling the three, and calling it "service.')

Second, because human beings are different from one another, it makes sense that what impresses each of us as true "service" will be as varied as the people receiving the treatment. However, our desire *to be served* as a part of doing business is something we all have in common!

Your best guide in creating the level of service your internal or external customers desire is found by simply asking yourself this important question:

> **If I were being taken care of as a customer exactly as I am treating *this* customer – would it make me feel good about doing business here?**

A "reality" television show in the United States, "Undercover Boss" shows a top executive going into disguise and working as a front-line employee at his or her own company – and having the opportunity to observe what really happens in the trenches in the organization.

(I have written previously how much I dislike this show – not because it isn't well-done or produced; but, instead, because I find it simply awful these executives aren't aware of what's happening at every level in the company in the first place!)

One show featured Michael Rubin, founder and CEO of GSI Commerce working unrecognized (at the company he had established as a teenager) in the "customer service" phone center – only to discover how rudely his own Customer Service Representatives (CSR) were talking to customers! One CSR said to Rubin words to the effect, "You can't waste time dealing with these people – all these customers want to do is complain!" (In fact, the customer was complaining about goods received in a damaged condition.)

Do you think for one instant this CSR would have accepted being on the receiving end of that kind of attitude if she were the customer and she received a damaged product? Of course not! If she had only asked herself the fundamental question of service – "If I was being taken care of as a customer exactly as I am treating *this* customer – would it make me feel good about doing business here?" – GSI Commerce would have a happy customer…and that CSR would still have her job!

(At the end of the segment on "Undercover Boss," it was stated the CSR entered a program where she was "retrained" – however, was no longer with the company.)

You must serve…as you would like to BE served.

"With"…

As stated earlier, when we say, "serve *with*," it means that merely to "serve" – while important -- is not quite enough. There must be a companion to that service to raise it to the level where it would assist us in progressing to an "ultimate customer experience."

Many people – and organizations – are willing to settle for "service." Not those, however, who seek to deliver the "ultimate customer experience." They are committed, and willing, to deliver more. They know that by doing more, they can be rewarded abundantly.

Doing well…by doing more!

Back in the 1980's, a 17-year-old young man knew the product he was selling for his summer job – newspaper subscriptions – was nothing truly extraordinary. However, he committed himself to the principle of doing something extra…in other words, the philosophy of "serve *with*."

He took it upon himself to go to his local City Hall, and literally write down by hand the mailing addresses of every new resident. He then sent each of them a warm welcome letter, and invited them to subscribe to the local newspaper so they could become more familiar with their new city.

Before the summer was over, he had earned tens of thousands of dollars and became the most successful newspaper subscription salesperson in his home state of Texas.

All by itself, this story is a great example of serving "*with.*" The young man made an extra effort – and, he also helped families discover more about, and probably become more comfortable in, their new place of residence. He took the time to welcome each of them personally, and they rewarded his initiative with their business.

However, there is one additional aspect to the story. This young man, inspired by his results, started his own business just a few years later, as a college student. Maybe you've heard of him: Michael Dell, founder of Dell Computers.

Again, notice that *everyone* can create an Ultimate Customer Experience, no matter where they work, or what they do...even a newspaper delivery boy!

When you serve customers, you help yourself!

When you become willing to add an ingredient to the service you deliver, you position yourself to do extraordinary good – for your organization, and yourself.

A multitude of studies on the topic of "job satisfaction" clearly state people are happier and more fulfilled in their careers when they are making a positive impact upon the people around them. (Do you believe the CSR mentioned earlier who was rude to customers had a high "job satisfaction" score? I don't. If you are displaying rude behavior to customers, you're probably also doing it to the colleagues working around you. How can you possibly be fulfilled to any degree at work when customers don't like you, and fellow employees want to avoid you?)

Maybe you won't become the founder of a large computer company – perhaps your choice is to continue to serve your current organization at your current position – however, not only will you become more valuable to your employer, you will find that your enjoyment and satisfaction at your job will be enhanced.

That's what happens when you "serve *with*"…

"Empathy"

If "service" isn't enough, and we are committed to serving "with" – what is the element we need to add to the mix?

It's *empathy*. As stated earlier, "empathy" is the act of identifying with the feelings of another person.

It's not the same as "sympathy" – which is sorrow for someone else's misfortunes. (Although, the way customers and colleagues are sometimes treated would perhaps rightly inspire some sympathy!)

While it tends to be on over-used example, one of the retail stores that I believe has done an extraordinary job in practicing this approach is Apple. When you enter an Apple store filled with enthusiasm to examine a new product, they do more than merely sell you an iPad. The employee sincerely shares your excitement. If you're frustrated over an inability to get a product to work in the manner you desire, they do more than give you the number for technical support. The team member at the "Genius Bar" connects with your irritation – and helps resolve your issue.

My friend, author and speaker Ross Schafer, says, "People do not want customer service as much as they desire customer *empathy*." I could not agree more. No one likes to feel all alone – we want, need, and desire to be connected. Serving the customer with empathy helps to create the connection we crave.

Empathy helps diffuse tough situations...

And, empathy is perhaps most important when dealing with customers who may be upset...or even angry. Remember, we all react to situations based upon our past experiences.

Since much of the time customers are disappointed in the level of connectivity they have at the places where they do business, they anticipate their expectations will be unfulfilled. In other words, many customers – mistreated and ill-served in previous situations – are betting you are going to let them down, even before you have had the opportunity to serve them. They are initiating their interaction with you with a "chip on their shoulder."

Emotional customers are often not rational people. You can't blame them for it – chances are you have been in a similar situation when you were an upset customer! A simple act of sincere empathy on your part can assist in diffusing the emotion of a difficult situation.

It's important to note: "Sincerity" is essential. If you are perceived to be phony, condescending, or not genuine in your communication, it could make an emotionally charged conversation become even more heated! When a telephone customer service agent says in a monotonous tone and insincere manner she "Appreciates how we feel" or "I would be happy to help you," it makes us feel exactly the *opposite* of the way the phrase was written to mean.

What can you say to display empathy? While you certainly wouldn't want to make any kind of admission that would have legal or ethical implications that could impact the company, to *sincerely* say to the customer, "I can see how that would disturb you!" Or, "I would certainly be upset if that happened to me, too!"

One of the all-time best is, "I apologize for this situation. It is certainly not up to our standards, or our usual performance. I will personally take care of this for you and correct the situation."

One recent morning I was checking email and digging into a couple of stories on the web, when my Internet connection went down.

Naturally, I run the drill where you unplug your cable modem and, when it fails to resolve the problem, I call technical service at my new Internet provider, Comcast. (The company is one of the largest providers of cable television in the United States.) The technician responds on the first ring, is very helpful, but tells me he has to transfer me to accounts receivable. I mention that it is impossible for me to have a "past due" bill, as I've been a subscriber for less than a month!

Imagine my surprise when the billing department comes on the line to tell me I've been disconnected because of an outstanding bill of over $2,000!

(Again, I tell them that would be difficult, as I have been a customer again for *less than one month*.)

The Customer Service Representative proceeds to inform me that about nine years ago, I failed to return equipment from a residence in Indianapolis – an address that I don't recall, especially since I was living in California at the time!

So, biting my tongue and holding my anger – remember, an upset customer isn't necessarily a rational one -- I asked:

1. *Why was I approved to receive my current service, if I owed them so much money?*
2. *Why did it take nine years to tell me?*
3. *How could I owe for equipment from a residence I wasn't living in at the time?*
4. *Why they didn't tell me about it before disconnecting me?*

Her response: "We sent you a letter on March 12."

Well, I didn't receive it...and since YOU are my phone company, too, did it occur to you to...here's an original idea...maybe use *your own service* to give me a call?

Now that both my Internet and phone service are down, I asked what could I do? According to her, the options were:

1) Pay the $2000+ dollars; or,

2) File a stolen identity report with the police, then file an affidavit with their company. The process, she said, usually takes over thirty days to complete. (Meaning more than a MONTH to get the web and a dial tone back.)

I asked for a supervisor...she said one would have to call me later.

Informing her that I would attempt to find a *nine-year-old* utility bill from California to show the location of my residence to prove I'm telling the truth -- and requesting just a thirty-day extension to resolve this matter, so I could have web access and a telephone to do so -- she coldly replied that I could pay the bill, or lose the service.

Fortunately, after posting my dilemma on Twitter,

@ComcastCares contacted me and started an investigation into the situation. Through Monica Ricci — a friend from a speech to National Association of Professional Organizers — I was put in touch with Reg Griffin, Vice President of Communications for Comcast for Southern Division. I was very impressed that once these folks found out, they immediately responded with empathy.

Less than an hour later, I received a call from Diane in the Comcast executive office saying they had researched the charge, found it erroneous and had wiped it off. AND…very importantly…Diane at Comcast *apologized*!

When Comcast disconnected my Internet and phone service because of a billing error, they failed at what we earlier described as Level One: Processing. When the customer service representative told me that she couldn't do anything because — even though Comcast had just installed new service at my house a couple of weeks earlier — she stated I had an outstanding bill of $2000 for unreturned equipment dating back about *nine years*!

(Even if it were true…which it isn't…what good would nine-year-old equipment be to them now, anyway?)

When I asked to speak to a supervisor, she told me none were available, but if I would leave my cell number (as Comcast had disconnected my home phone), someone would call. No one ever did. Again, a major failure at Level One.

Fortunately, social media in the form of Twitter came to my rescue. To say Comcast's response was prompt would be an understatement…to suggest it was impressive would be minimizing its significance. The Twitter Team at Comcast jumped on the issue, and help was on the way.

It's important to note, Comcast displayed they understood the importance of Level Two: Service. Not only did they correct their Processing error, they engaged me with empathy. The most important aspect of all of this to me was this simple fact: I really felt the next level at Comcast did something vitally important. They sincerely cared. It diffused my anger toward the situation and the company – and created a thrilled customer.

Later, some people commented my resolution occurred so rapidly because I have about 80,000 Twitter followers and a successful blog. Perhaps that's the case – frankly, I'm naive about that stuff. I honestly got the feeling they wanted to correct a situation and keep a customer happy -- because that is the best, and most profitable, way to run any business.

However, a great lesson for ALL organizations is to reaffirm the primary importance of the person who has initial contact with customers "serving with empathy." It should never get to the point where jumping on social media and enlisting the aid of your followers is necessary to attain results. If a CSR handles the situation — and is given the authority to do so — it prevents major headaches! Ever noticed many times when a company corrects an error, they don't say they are sorry? Here, Comcast handled it exactly right after higher levels became involved.

If a flight attendant offers me a hot cup of coffee on a smooth, on-time flight, that's Level Two: Service. If the airline fails at Level One: Processing – in other words, if the flight is four hours late, I'm going to miss my connection and be stranded overnight – I don't really care about how hot or good the coffee may be. However, once we are Processed perfectly – once you "get it right" – then, taking it up to Level Two: Service (and "Serve With Empathy") makes a powerful impact upon the customers with whom you interact.

People make mistakes. Policies get misaligned. However, when good folks can step in, show they care, and serve with empathy on behalf of the customer in a sincere manner, people like me are willing to continue to send you checks!

What can happen when we fail to be empathetic...

I'm more aware than ever before that at every business, every customer now has a big microphone and a huge platform!

At a recent speech I presented before an audience of well over 1,000, the CEO of the company I was addressing announced they had changed the "official airline" of the convention from United Airlines to Delta Airlines.

Then, he said, "Here's the reason." Turning to the huge screens on the wall, he played a song from YouTube, "United Breaks Guitars."

According to the website, HuffingtonPost.com, "Nearly 4 million people have watched the 'United Breaks Guitars' video that has made its way around the web and back." (In fact, as of this writing in 2013, the viewing count has now exceeded 13 million!) "United Airlines passenger Dave Carroll had his Taylor guitar destroyed by the airline's baggage handlers during a flight last year. After United repeatedly declined to reimburse him for the damage, he wrote a now-famous song decrying their customer service and their brand. It was funny, justified and smart. The damage to United's brand was undeniable."

In an article from July 2009, in "The Times" of London, Chris Ayres wrote, "If there's one person in America who you wouldn't want to be right now, it is Ms. Irlweg. You see, several months ago, Ms. Irlweg had the misfortune of handling a passenger complaint from a man named Dave Carroll, who happens to be a Canadian musician with a lethally dry sense of humor. Carroll had been flying on United when he saw baggage handlers throwing around his guitar case on the tarmac outside, and when he arrived at his destination, it turned out that the neck of his beloved $3,500 Taylor six-string had been snapped. But when he asked for compensation, he was fobbed off by department after department, until finally he reached Ms. Irlweg, who at least gave him a straight answer: 'No.'"

The article continues, "'Fine,' he said to her, 'But I'm going to write three songs about my experience with your airline, shoot videos for each of them, and then post them online.' Yeah, right, she must have been thinking. But Carroll kept his promise."

Ayres goes on to report that following the public relations disaster caused by millions of people watching such a negative video about the airline, United's stock fell by ten percent – a loss of $180,000,000 in value! (Or, to put it another way, the price of more than 51,000 replacement guitars.)

At the meeting I was attending, the corporate CEO of my client stated, if United "will be as unresponsive to a customer as they were to that guy, they're not going to be OUR airline!"

The travel for the one thousand people attending that convention was just a minor part of the cost United had to pay for service without empathy.

Contrast, however, the damage done to United Airlines with what happened to Taxi Terry – whom I made a video about that runs on YouTube, as well. Terry has picked up convention and individual business from many people who watched my story on his service with empathy. His business is growing and thriving, even in a challenging economy.

> **You make the fundamental choice. You can be Ms. Irlweg...or, Taxi Terry.**

The importance of serving with empathy – as a major component in creating an "Ultimate Customer Experience" -- for our customers is more important now than ever. If customers complain, as in the case with United and the musician – or if customers are thrilled, as I was with Taxi Terry – you must remember that in today's connected marketplace…the whole world is watching!

UCE Checklist

1. How would YOU define "serve"?
   a. Can you give an example outside of your job where you have been of service?
2. How about "empathy"?
   a. Can you provide an example outside of the place where you work where someone displayed empathy to you?
3. Remember the critical question of this chapter:
   > i. **If I were being taken care of as a customer exactly as I am treating *this* customer – would it make me feel good about doing business here?**
   b. What percentage of the time are you taking care of customers (remember, we're talking about BOTH internal and external customers!) exactly like you would prefer to be served?
   c. What would you have to do to increase that figure to 100%?
4. Bert Boeckmann said we cannot work "just" for a paycheck and truly serve the customer.
   a. Other than compensation, what do *you* work for?
5. What could Comcast have done better in their dealings with me?
6. What should have United done to prevent the musician from making the YouTube videos?

Step Four: Connect With Emotion

We've defined Level One as Processing – the basic elements essential to the transaction that a customer has every right to expect.

Level Two is Service – those steps we take to assist, engage, and serve the customer with empathy so the elements of Processing do not feel impersonal and robotic.

Now, it's time to take it up to Level Three: Experience.

The customer experience is a higher level than customer service, because the experience enhances the interaction you have with the customer to the point it is perceived to be both personal and emotional. That's why Step Four in creating the Ultimate Customer Experience is to "Connect With Emotion."

Let's face it; emotion is a very challenging topic to address in business. Sometimes, this issue revolves around gender stereotypes. Men often state they do not want to engage in emotion in the professional arena, because it may make them appear to be weak and vulnerable. Women have suggested in several studies they can often be reticent to connect with customers and colleagues emotionally, because it can be perceived as showing a lack of the aggressiveness and ambition supposedly required for professional success.

So, from the outset, let me make it clear that by stating we need to "Connect With Emotion," I am NOT suggesting we become a pushover, weeping and wailing with customers over their personal situations. Connecting emotionally does *not* mean engaging overly intimately, or inappropriately.

It means we are going to, for example, concern ourselves with not only how our product works, but also how it makes the customer feel to use it. We are going to concentrate not only on what results our service delivers, but also what compelling impact it creates.

Taking it higher...

As I sat in the wrecked automobile, the dust from the air bag was covering my suit. My ears still ringing from the shotgun-like sound of its deployment, I pried opened my car door and limped to the driver in the car I had just struck to make certain he was uninjured.

After calling the police – and still more than a little unsteady from the accident – I realized there was another telephone call I needed to make. I was driving a rental car from Hertz.

Finding my cell phone on the floorboard of the automobile, I pulled the car rental agreement from the glove compartment and found the number I knew was listed there, but that I had never in my over-twenty years of renting cars previously been required to use.

I knew the words on the folder almost perfectly: "If you're in an accident, first call the police -- then call this number." I had called the police – now it was time to call Hertz and tell them I had just totaled one of their cars.

"This is Hertz," the kind voice on the other end of the line answered. "How may I help you?"

"Well, I hate to tell you this – I have never had to make one of these calls before – but I've just wrecked my rental car." Robotically, as if in a surreal dream state, I read the rental record number from the agreement, told her the exact spot on the highway the accident had happened, and started to inform her I needed a wrecker for the car, a ride to the airport to catch a later flight home, and assistance with the accident claim. However, before I could get that all out – and just after she had the record number – she interrupted.

"Mr. McKain – I understand. *Sir, first off...are you alright?*"

"Yes, ma'am, I'm fine. Thanks for asking." With my foggy state of consciousness, it wasn't until later I realized she knew my name because I gave her the rental record number, and she had all of my information on the screen in front of her. Once again, I attempted my request for a wrecker for the car, a ride to the airport to catch a later flight home, and assistance with the accident claim.

My head was throbbing from the combination of the accident, the heat of the afternoon and the stress of the traffic jam that had been caused during rush hour in New York City by the wreck.

(Suffice it to say that the hand gestures directed my way and elicited by the accident were not out of a civic concern for my health.)

"Mr. McKain...are you *absolutely certain* that you are OK?" the Hertz representative persisted.

"Well – I am a little wobbly right now, but I'm not injured."

"I want you to be completely, absolutely positive that you are uninjured," she said. "Hertz can always get another car – *but we can NEVER get another Mr. McKain.*"

That was the instant when Hertz transcended from customer service to a customer experience – from "Serving With Empathy" to "Connecting With Emotion" – on the way to an Ultimate Customer Experience.

Notice how perfectly she followed the Three Levels of Customer Interaction:

She Processed – and Got It Right – all of the information and my accident situation. She did everything I had a right, as a customer, to expect from Hertz.

She Served With Empathy. Practically the first words she said to me after learning of the accident were, "I understand."

She Connected With Emotion. The moment she convinced me Hertz cared more about ME than they did their own CARS, I became a customer for life!

My friend, fellow speaker, and author of several terrific books, including "The Likability Factor," Tim Sanders, said it perfectly: "Organizations need to deliver not only high-quality products and services, but also staged experiences that are dramatic and engaging. It's no longer about highlighting benefits -- it's about creating sensations." Hertz created a sensation – an emotion – for me. The result is that I've been back and literally spent tens of thousands of dollars with them!

It's a personality contest!

What if I were to tell you one of the most emotionally connected brands in the United States was the "Government Employees Auto Insurance Corporation"? You would probably shake your head in disbelief, right? Few aspects of life sound as boring as insuring your car, and, unfortunately, there are few employees we encounter more emotionally disconnected from their customers than the ones who work for the governments of our respective countries.

Yet, in the US, if I would show literally ANY person a picture of a caveman...or a cute talking gecko...(the "spokespersons" for hilarious advertising campaigns) and say the acronym the company is known by – GEICO – it would elicit immediate recognition, and perhaps most importantly, a smile!

The leaders of the Government Employees Auto Insurance Corporation realized – quite rightly – as they sought to expand their base beyond exclusively employees of the various levels of government, the perception in the marketplace generated by their name would fail to connect emotionally with potential customers. As Brian McManus, a senior account executive at Springboard Public Relations in Marlboro, New Jersey, has noted, "GEICO had established itself as a solid brand through superior service and consistently lower rates. With the solid foundation in place, the company was able to be very aggressive with its personality (marketing) campaign. GEICO has done such a good job of making us laugh, that we just want to be around them, and we want to do business with them."

Note that McManus points out the company had already provided superior service. However, by taking it to a higher level and connecting emotionally with customers, it became one of the most successful in its industry in the entire nation.

Connecting with emotion works for *individuals* – as it did for me with the woman from Hertz after my wreck – and it works for *organizations* – as it has for GEICO in the enormously competitive world of auto insurance. And, if YOU will connect emotionally with the customers and prospects you serve, it will work for you and your organization, as well!

Three steps to connection...

So, how do you go about emotionally connecting with customers?

There is a three-step process involved – and, my bet is it will seem very familiar to you. It's the same way you connect with individuals of significance in your personal life. Perhaps you haven't thought of it in this manner – you didn't break down the process of getting acquainted and dating someone who became a significant other into three-steps, for example – however, it's always important to keep reminding ourselves that customers…just like us…are people! Therefore, the behaviors and emotions we have noticed others display in our personal lives are identical to the behaviors and emotions we will see them display in our professional relationships.

The three steps are:

1. *Align*
2. *Engage*
3. *Commit*

Align

Why would a customer do business with you? There has to be a fundamental reason, or else they would be staying at home – or, at least spending their money elsewhere. What need drives them to look at your organization as an option? What motivates them to make the effort to engage with you?

What's important to an internal customer? Why would there be a conflict at work with a colleague?

Once you know the answer to those questions, you can begin the process of alignment.

I've often heard it said in our personal lives, "opposites attract." Over my years of observing – as well as being in – personal relationships, my conclusion is that while they may attract, they often have a difficult time of enduring!

Instead, we tend to associate most with people we perceive to be like us! Personal relationships flourish when there are common areas of interest. Don't get me wrong, I'm not saying you have to like everything your partner likes – or vice versa. It's that our common interests, values, and desires pull us together...while our differences make the relationship interesting!

When you can align your thinking with another, you begin to appreciate and understand them more deeply. I am *not* suggesting you have to adopt their choices or beliefs – instead, I am strongly recommending to connect emotionally with another, you must (at least temporarily) be able to approximately think as they think, choose as they choose, feel as they feel.

It would not be over-reaching to suggest this simple act is at the basis of many of the world's problems, and has been for centuries. Because of our unwillingness, or inability, to even temporarily align our thinking with those of another religion, ethnic background, culture, or national experience, we act and communicate in a way others from different experiences fail to comprehend.

Here is an important point: **People rarely behave irrationally!**

People almost always behave rationally – *from their point of view!*

My wife will come home loaded down with shopping bags from purchases at the mall. I go crazy! "How could you spend all that money?" I'll ask desperately.

She will smile sweetly, hold the bags higher, and announce, "I saved us so much money today!"

"HOW?" I ask, perplexed.

And, of course, she replies confidently, "I bought all of this...ON

SALE!"

Who is right?

(When I ask this at seminars, men will typically shout, "YOU are!" Women declare, "SHE is!")

The answer is…we BOTH are! From our own respective point of view.

As the person in our family in charge of the budget, I am rational and correct to be highly concerned about expenditures. As the person with most of the responsibility of buying clothes and school supplies for the children, she naturally looks for savings on her purchases.

For me, it is entirely correct to get emotional about how much she is spending. For her, it is entirely correct to get emotional about how much she is saving.

The fundamentally important aspect here is that if she seeks to influence my thinking and my emotions, she must first align with my point of view and communicate with me from that basis. To simply keep insisting she saved us money because the items she purchased were discounted won't persuade me.

However, once she begins to come from my perspective – "Honey, I know you are worried about our finances. These are items you have already been thorough enough to have already considered – and, I was able to spend less than we anticipated for items we were going to need to acquire anyway!" – she has won the day!

It doesn't mean she has to change her beliefs! It just means to be effective at the next stage – engage -- she needs to first align her thinking to a point where I feel we are connected.

Engage

Notice, my wife won the day when she aligned, then engaged. What good would it do for her to align – to make the effort to understand my perspective – then, just keep it all to herself?

However, also note that to engage without aligning would not have accomplished what she desired!

If she would have said, "You don't understand. The sale was FIFTY percent off! It's *half* of what it normally would have been," it wouldn't have engaged me, because we weren't aligned. The problem is, without the alignment, I would have been hearing, "You don't understand. Because it was on sale, I spent money I didn't need to spend – and, because it was half-off, *I bought twice as much!"*

People respond more enthusiastically and productively when they are engaged. According to an article in the June 2007 issue of "CFO Magazine," electronic retailer Best Buy reports, "where employee engagement increases by a 0.1 (on a five-point scale), (the store) experiences a $100,000 increase in annual sales." If you can create Ultimate Internal Customer Experiences, these results indicate you'll stimulate enhanced revenue.

My very good friend, noted author and speaker Joe Calloway, often asks audiences if they can guess his favorite restaurant. After a few attempts by the audience – who always respond with the name of a specific eatery – Calloway makes a terrific point. He says, "My favorite restaurant is the one where they know my name."

The American patriot, Benjamin Franklin, wrote, "The sweetest sound in any language is a man's own name." Today, he would probably suggest the most compelling sound in any native tongue is when a man or woman is recognized by someone, and called by his or her own name with genuine sincerity.

When you break that down, you begin to realize the only way Joe Calloway realizes they know his name is because someone at the restaurant has *used* it! I might know your name, but until I recognize you by name in a conversation, YOU don't know that I know it.

Not only did someone at the restaurant make the effort to understand something important to Joe – remembering our earlier point about a person's name, and having that knowledge makes one feel important, which assists in alignment – an individual actually engaged Joe by using his name in a conversation.

In today's world of marketing, there is a significant amount of discussion on the term "engagement" – what it means, and how to measure it.

For our purpose here in creating an Ultimate Customer Experience, the word "engagement" means one precise thing: You make the effort to create and sustain interaction with customers.

Commit

Let's say you are engaged with every kid on a local sports team. You align with them, because you understand a bit about the challenges they are facing as they learn a sport and compete with other teams. You engage them, as you call each by his or her name, share a smile and some encouragement, and attempt to keep their spirits high.

Every young person on the team is pretty terrific. However, one of the kids is your daughter. To you, which person on the team is the most special?

Pretty obvious, right? While you are aligned and engaged with every young person, you have a commitment to your own child that runs deeper than words can describe. That commitment you have makes all of the difference.

To be blunt, there is no way you will ever possess – or should have – a commitment to a customer as strong as your bond with your offspring. However, this example should illuminate that when there is true commitment, there is additional – and significant – emotional intensity.

In our personal lives, we have acquaintances, friends, and true commitments. With individuals with whom we have shared commitments – whether it is romantic or platonic – we develop a higher level of concentration upon making certain we have contributed to their well-being in a positive, productive manner.

It's a similar phenomenon when we display a commitment to our customers. We simply develop and display a higher level of concentration and intensity toward creating an experience that contributes to their personal and professional success.

The woman from Hertz aligned with me after my car accident. She engaged me in conversation to be certain I was not injured. However, when she displayed a personal and organizational commitment to me, she hooked me as a customer for life! This triad of "align, engage, and commit" worked perfectly to create a loyal advocate for her company.

Here's an interesting aspect about commitment: We want it to be returned, and often we want to return it.

If you are in a monogamous personal relationship, you probably insist the other person has a reciprocal standard. In other words, if you are faithful…they had better not be cheating! When we extend a commitment, we desire it to be returned at approximately the same level.

When you consider a recent study quoted by Fred Reichheld in his book, "Loyalty Rules" that found most companies *lose HALF of their customers* in a five-year period, you can see that a lack of reciprocal commitment in the business world has a profound impact upon the financial success of your organization.

In any true relationship where you find a degree of commitment, there is a *reciprocal loyalty.*

You count on your spouse to be faithful, just as he or she expects the same from you. You depend upon friends and family to provide emotional support when you need it – and you stand ready to do the same for them.

The Josephson Institute of Ethics states there are "six pillars of character" in making ethical choices and building committed, emotionally connected relationships. Those six are:

1. *Trustworthiness*
2. *Respect*
3. *Responsibility*
4. *Fairness*
5. *Caring*
6. *Citizenship*

The Institute states a hallmark of "Trustworthiness" is someone who understands the importance of loyalty and appreciates it is higher calling than merely "looking out for others."

You cannot be loyal to a group or individual – and display the other "pillars of character" such as "caring" and "respect" -- if you do not have *their* best interests at heart. That's achieved with alignment, engagement, and commitment.

People understand this principle innately – and somehow just "know" when you do not have genuine concern for their needs and wants. Somewhere along the way we intuitively understand when a business is more concerned about selling their stuff than helping our situation. We know when a person we work with has our back – and when they are just saying they do, but can't be trusted to follow through.

Front door – back door

Prospecting is really the attempt by any business to attract new customers, isn't it? Every organization wants to expand its client base and grow the business -- obviously there is nothing wrong with that -- in fact it is mandatory. Your company *needs* to have your front door open…in other words, to take the necessary steps to bring new customers inside!

The problem, however, is many companies fail to examine two important points:

- First, how do the methods of customer acquisition set the *tone* for the experience that they will expect once they pass through the "front door?" (It's the "first impression" we discussed earlier.)
- Second, what *happens* to these customers once they are inside? (It's "connecting with emotion" once they are there.)

To put it another way, many organizations have the front door open, but are using tricks and techniques to get customers to come inside instead of forming (by connecting with emotion and creating an Ultimate Customer Experience) the foundation of a loyal, long term customer relationship.

AND, organizations have been focusing so much on the front door, they haven't noticed that the back door is wide open – and customers are streaming out!

Here's an obvious point – but one that, for some reason, so many organizations seem to be missing: *It doesn't matter how many new customers you are bringing in the front, if you're losing more out the back!*

In my first book, I discussed how all organizations have a "recruitment" strategy for finding new employees, but significantly fewer have a "retention" strategy for keeping and growing the employees they've brought on board. Now, I'm suggesting to you that the SAME principle applies to the manner in which many businesses deal with customers!

As the late Dr. Kenneth McFarland, one of the early of professional business speakers in the United States, often remarked, when you think about it, the only thing any advertisement really represents is an *invitation* to go through the sponsor's front door. You'll see countless ads from businesses wanting you -- their prospect -- to come inside. These same companies often have not a clue how to develop the *experiences* that engender loyalty with a customer they've just acquired.

(It's like the old line about the dog chasing cars – he wouldn't know what to do if he ever *caught* one!)

Yet, because many businesses will center their activities upon acquisition instead of retention – on prospecting instead of loyalty – on transactions instead of experiences -- they create a huge disconnection between what customers are truly seeking and what their organization is offering.

You can change that. The next step centers upon your role in making this connection happen – regardless of the industry or specific organization where you work.

It's difficult – I would even suggest it is *impossible* – to become loyal and engaged as a customer, an employee…simply as a human being…to anyone or anything without feeling emotionally connected.

If you desire to create Ultimate Customer Experiences, you have to align, engage, and commit...you must connect with emotion.

UCE Checklist

1. Imagine a customer in distress, much like I was after my accident in the rental car from Hertz.
   a. What would your "company policy" be in regards to a customer in that situation?
   b. What, from your perspective, SHOULD be the response to a customer having such a challenging time?
      i. Identify and explore the differences between the policy and what would be best for the customer, if any.
2. What is an example where you have practiced "alignment" to better understand someone else's perspective?
   a. How did it influence the manner in which you communicated with them?
   b. How did it change or enhance your perspective?
3. Name a time you made a personal effort to engage someone that otherwise you might have simply left them alone.
   a. How did they feel after you made the effort?
   b. How did YOU feel after extending yourself in such a manner?
4. Where do you shop or do business where the organization you are purchasing from conveys a commitment to their customers?
   a. How does it impact how you feel about the business?
   b. What could you and your organization do to make your customers feel in a similar manner?
5. Name three things your organization – and you – do to make certain you retain your current customers.
   a. If you cannot think of three – get to work to create more steps to keeping the customers you already have!
      i. Without customers, there is no

business…and without businesses, there are no jobs!

Step Five: Take Personal Responsibility

Both resorts are in Hawaii…one on the island of Kauai, the other Maui. Both are pretty close to the definition of paradise. At the time my wife and I visited – a couple of years ago -- both properties could have used some "freshening." They looked a little dated…the carpets worn, the furniture scuffed, the hallways dinged.

At the hotel in Maui, a room service tray evidently from the previous occupants of our room sat in the hall for two days. A part of the shower was broken. A light bulb in the bathroom was out and never replaced. The "This Elevator Up" sign at one station in the lobby was broken with what appeared to be exposed wiring. Our bed was made each day, but the room wasn't really cared for…the ironing board remained out, trash remained in the can. They were failing at Level One: Processing.

After I accidently left my key in the room, I went to the front desk with my ID to ask for another. I gently reminded the desk clerk to be certain that I also had access to the 22nd floor Club, for which I qualified as a frequent guest of that particular hotel chain.

"No, you don't," she stated. "It's nowhere on your record you have access." I softly explained that I had the gold sticker on my key, and my wife and I had previously been to the club on this trip.

"No, you haven't," she argued. "It is nowhere in here that you qualify."

"Well," I asked as politely as I could, "then how do I know about the gold sticker on the key?"

"You must have seen someone else's."

(OK...here's my question...even if I DON'T qualify, WHY would you have such an argument with a customer who is already paying you pretty high rates when all the hotel would be out is a couple cups of coffee and slices of pineapple? Why not TAKE THE CUSTOMER'S WORD? What can possibly be gained by winning the argument?)

When I returned to my room, I found my old key *with the sticker*, and — for the heck of it — went back to the front desk and simply said, "I wanted you to see this so you would know I was telling you the truth."

Believe it or not, her response was, "Well, I have no idea how YOU got THAT!"

I took laundry to the bell desk my first morning at the Maui hotel, only to be told by another woman there, "We normally come and pick that up."

"Oh..." I responded with a smile, "well...I saved you the trip!"

Her response? "Hmmmmph." No "thank you" — or "you shouldn't have" or "I'm calling security on you!" Nothing but "Hmmmmph."

At the Maui resort, I have a feeling the (not too) subtle attitude is, "We have a great view of the ocean. We even have penguins in the lobby! If you wanted service, go someplace else. We don't have to work too hard with real estate like this."

Meanwhile, at the then-Princeville Hotel in Kauai, the bellman apologized for the hotel's wear and tear, but vowed, "We are going to make sure you have a FABULOUS stay!" (It reminded me of Taxi Terry asking if I was ready for the "best cab ride of my life?")

He engaged us in conversation. He asked several questions: How long had we been married? Was this a honeymoon? How many times had we been to Hawaii? His sincere and engaging manner did not make his inquiries feel intrusive – rather, he seemed truly interested in us as people, not merely customers from whom he sought a tip.

He then told us the story of how he came to Hawaii for vacation – and never returned to Pennsylvania!

Connecting at a higher level...

It's important to note – when you are at Level Two and serving with empathy, the conversation will be about eighty percent listening, and twenty percent talking. (Obviously, that's a broad statement that can vary based upon the specific situation and the unique product or service you offer.)

However, when you enter the higher level of connecting with emotion at Level Three, the communication will tend to be more of a fifty-fifty proposition. Connection is reciprocal, as we have learned. The bellman began with Processing – getting our luggage on the cart, learning our room number, and assisting us to the elevator. Next, he was providing Service with Empathy – listening about our travels, our disappointment with the Maui hotel, sharing our excitement for a vacation in Hawaii. Lastly, he Connected with Emotion. By revealing his story, and sharing a laugh – humor is an emotional response – he was moving us to feel as if we had a new friend, a true personal connection.

Later that same day, as we checked in for the hotel's luau, the man behind the registration table — named Doug — welcomed us enthusiastically and sincerely. He, too, engaged us in conversation, asking in-depth questions about our initial impressions of their property.

The next morning, after working out in the hotel gym, Tammy and I went over to the bar to order a smoothie, only to notice Doug was working behind the bar. Immediately he smiled and said…and this is a *quote*…"Hey! Good morning to the McKain's!"

Are you kidding me? He remembered our names?

The following morning it was, "Good morning, Scott! Good morning, Tammy!" He told us the hotel was going to be undergoing renovation — moving up to a St. Regis brand after all of the remodeling work was done. His enthusiasm for the future of the resort made an impact.

We should always remember this important aspect: **Emotion is contagious.** If you choose to be sincerely enthusiastic about engaging your customers, don't be surprised when customers are excited about interacting with you. When you put your best foot forward, even with the people with whom you work on a daily basis, you build a spirit of teamwork. On the other hand, if you decide to remain distant from the customers and colleagues of your organization, you should not be shocked when they are aloof and disconnected from you. It's why taking personal responsibility – for your attitude, as well as for your interaction with the customer – is so extraordinarily important.

Obviously, neither of these Hawaiian hotels was going to go bankrupt without our business. Both were pretty full on the February week when we were guests. I realize their future was not dependent upon our choice to stay with them.

However, at the end of the day, it's NOT about your location…it's about the experience you create. I wouldn't return to the Maui hotel -- even for a much cheaper rate. However, we're saving up for a return trip to see the now-St. Regis in

Princeville — even though it's obviously going to cost us a lot more our next trip.

You see, although the sign on the front and the décor had yet to be upgraded to read "St. Regis," the hotel already had elite caliber people like Doug working at the resort.

In Maui, the hotel isn't the only thing that needs refreshing.

Notice, both properties were a little "worn" at the time we were guests. However, the *people* created the experience in Kauai, because they took the **personal responsibility** to connect with us.

To bring the story full circle – and to provide another example of how Hertz has connects with customers -- while driving in Kauai, my cell phone rang with a caller marked "Unknown." I answered to a recording from Hertz that basically wondered when I was going to return my Maui rental car. The problem is…I already had checked it in several days earlier!

When we checked out of the hotel in Maui, the Hertz desk was closed, so I asked the bellman taking our luggage to the airport transport shuttle if he could help me get the car returned. He told me he would take care of it…and I tipped him for his trouble.

Somehow, he didn't get the car returned — and Hertz was holding me responsible. (Which, of course, is what you would *expect* them to do!)

When I called the hotel in Maui and was connected with the bell desk, I explained the situation. I told the woman on the line that a bell captain said he could get the car taken care of – when she interrupted and announced, "We don't have bell captains working at that hour!"

I asked, more than a bit incredulous, "You don't have bell staff then? Who helped me with my luggage?"

She responded, "We have bellmen working twenty-four hours -- but there are no *CAPTAINS* on duty then!"

I tried to politely explain that I wasn't familiar with their unique terminology, but felt the issue was more about a missing automobile than hotel titles at that point. Then I realized...this was the *same* woman I encountered during my problem with the key! She, once again, was less than helpful...and rude.

I called the Hertz desk again at the Maui hotel, and connected with a customer service representative. He promised to figure out what was wrong — and make it right.

Not long after, he called me back to keep me posted. He hadn't found the car, or even the keys, but he wanted me to know that he was still working on it.

Another hour later, he called with the good news. He found the car, and since it was not my fault, there would be no additional charges for the days that Hertz didn't have the car. He asked if there was any additional way he could assist us. My relief at the discovery of the car, and the waiving of charges, was an emotional connection. And, another example of why I am such a fan of Hertz...and why we will never return to the hotel in Maui.

Just stop and think...

Could you imagine for a moment that Taxi Terry would ever allow a customer to become as frustrated with his service as I became with the hotel desk clerk? It's impossible for me to even consider! The reason is because Terry takes personal responsibility for his efforts in dealing with customers.

It's all a matter of choice. The woman at the desk in Maui *chose* to behave in the manner she did.

How are you choosing to deal with the internal and external customers at your organization? Are you the Maui desk clerk...or Taxi Terry?

Don't get me wrong – I've heard all the excuses:

- *"If you had to deal with the customers we put up with..."*
- *"Management has cut back staff so much, it's all I can do to get my work done, never mind putting up with customers!"*
- *"If you had to work in weather like I do..."*
- *"Hey, I'm just a part-timer here. Customer service isn't my job."*
- *"Nobody trained me on how to deal with customers."*
- *"I am under so much pressure here, you can't expect someone with my level of stress to be nice ALL of the time!"*
- *"Nobody else here cares about customers, why should I?"*

On and on the excuses go...

And, that's all they are – lame excuses by individuals who, for some unknown reason, prefer the choice to be an unhelpful, rude jerk...rather than choose to take personal responsibility and create Ultimate Customer Experiences.

Dietrich Bonhoffer wrote, ""Action springs not from thought, but from a readiness for responsibility." The point for you is simple: You aren't ready to take action until you first have taken personal responsibility.

The esteemed research foundation, The Brookings Institution, provided this definition of "personal responsibility": "Personal responsibility is the willingness to both accept the importance of standards that society establishes for individual behavior and to make strenuous personal efforts to live by those standards."

Pretty powerful, isn't it? You not only make the decision to accept the standards – in other words, creating the kinds of experiences for customers you desire for yourself when you're in a similar position – you are also willing to make a "strenuous personal effort" to deliver!

However, the report continues, "But personal responsibility also means that when individuals fail to meet expected standards, **they do not look around for some factor outside themselves to blame.** The demise of personal responsibility occurs when individuals blame their family, their peers, their economic circumstances, or their society for their own failure to meet standards." (emphasis added)

Throwing your colleagues, the company, your personal problems, the economy, your family, the competition – *whatever*! – under the proverbial bus as an excuse for your failure to create an Ultimate Customer Experience is the most obvious sign of a lack of personal responsibility!

To assist you in developing the readiness to take personal responsibility, let's begin with this reminder of two things the customer experience is NOT:

1. There is NOT a "customer service department" or "customer experience department"
2. The customer experience is NOT an activity exclusively delegated to others in the organization

First, there should never be a "department" in charge of handling the service of customers, for this important reason: EVERYONE should view themselves as vital in – and responsible for -- creating Ultimate Customer Experiences.

Therefore, if the company where you work has a "department" in charge of customers, you should understand they may have a primary role in the interaction your organization has with its customers – but, they are *never* the exclusive owner of the relationship!

As we stated from the beginning, in every organization there are internal and external customers. No matter your position – from front lines to CEO – you are serving some type of customer, regardless of the department in which you work.

One time, the Chief Financial Officer of a major company mentioned the content of my speech on customer experiences had "nothing to do" with him, as he was CFO and had "no customer responsibilities." I couldn't believe someone with such a limited perspective had attained such a significant position! First of all, those very finances he was directing were obtained because customers were spending money on their products and services. If you aren't passionate about your current customers spending more money with you – and obtaining new customers to enhance revenue and profitability – how can you truly be the "chief financial" *anything*?

Hey, if my job literally depended upon customers spending money with us, I would be passionate and engaged about this – wouldn't *you*?

Good.

Because, it does.

No matter your responsibilities with your organization, sooner or later, your very employment depends upon **you** taking personal responsibility for creating Ultimate Customer Experiences for the internal and external customers in your company.

Circuit City was a major electronics retailer in the United States for many years. I will wager there existed employees in the payroll department, for example, who could swear their job had nothing to do with customers being thrilled and returning to purchase more.

Yet, when customers stopped coming to Circuit City, it wasn't just the salespeople on the floor who lost their jobs when the company went bankrupt.

Am I suggesting if one person in the payroll department took personal responsibility, created UCE's for the internal customers on her team, and applied these principles that Circuit City might have survived?

Maybe. It only takes one person to stand up and be counted to make a meaningful difference.

However, in all likelihood, it would not have saved the company. Here's what it *would* do…that single, amazing, personally responsible professional would have created so much goodwill as a result of her actions, other worthy companies would want her on their team. And, she would be given the opportunity to work with people who "get it" the way she does – and the lives of colleagues and customers would be enhanced and enriched as a result.

If Taxi Terry couldn't drive a cab anymore, do you think he would have any trouble getting a great job? I don't! I know there are lots of his customers who would love to have someone of his ability and integrity on their team. Wouldn't you love to work with someone as creative and compelling?

If the operator at Hertz called my company and asked for a job, don't you know she would move to the front of the line? Of course!

The point is, great results happen for your organization when you take personal responsibility – however, it pales in comparison when you measure the return you will receive, individually, for doing so.

What do I do?

Let's imagine you haven't been the best at taking personal responsibility for creating Ultimate Customer Experiences. What should you do to get on the right track?

Ironically, to get ON the right track, you first must STOP riding on the current one. Here's a quick checklist:

STOP blaming others. When you catch yourself saying, "It's not my fault," and suggesting someone else is culpable, stop! This isn't to suggest you become a martyr and think every problem is yours! It IS to say you accept your fair share of responsibility – and leave it to others to assign blame.

STOP making excuses. Really…just quit reciting them. When you claim you just can't get ahead…or you had awful parents…or you really didn't have a choice…or your genes are bad…all you do is seem lame. Whether you realize it or not, ALL of us have had something happen in our lives that would create the fodder for a pile of stale justifications. When you make yours, it does nothing to alleviate your situation. It just makes you look like you are shirking your responsibility in the process.

STOP whining. One of my best friends in the world, Larry Winget, wrote a great book with a terrific title: "Shut Up, Stop Whining, and Get A Life!" See the points in the previous paragraph. The same goes here.

STOP seeing the cloud around the silver lining. Ever know someone who could make a room seem brighter because they *left it?* People detest association with constant negativity. When you project "nothing is going to work," or that "everything is doomed," the negative energy you emit will repel people from you. Does bad stuff happen? Sure, it does…even to really great people. I'm sure Michael J. Fox didn't desire Parkinson's disease…the late Christopher Reeve would have preferred the accident that made him a quadriplegic had never happened. Yet, in spite of their circumstances, both men found ways to triumph, in part by taking responsibility for their future. You should apply the principles from their example.

STOP waiting for things to happen. I love the old story about a man in his house when a major flood began. A policeman told him to go to higher ground, but the man said no. "God will take care of me," he assured them.

As the water was rising to his doorstep, two firemen in a rescue boat docked at his home and pleaded with him to leave with them. The man said no. "God will take care of me," he assured them.

The flooding overtaking his home, the man climbed onto the roof of his house. A helicopter circled overhead, dropping a rope to pull the man to safety. The man said no, and refused the rope. "God will take care of me," he assured them.

The man drowned.

Entering Heaven, the man was angry with God! He challenged Him, saying, "How could you let me down when I waited for you and put my trust in you?"

God replied, "I sent a policeman, two firemen, and a helicopter. What more did you want?"

People who fail to take action on their own are those who fail to take personal responsibility – and vice versa.

It's like writing a book. There is only one way to do it – you put the seat of your pants in the seat of a chair and write. The world is full of would-be authors who are waiting for inspiration from the universe to begin. Which is the reason there are more would-be authors than real-life authors…more people wait for things to happen than make things happen.

Ultimate Customer Experiences don't happen unless someone – *exactly like YOU* – stops waiting for things to happen, and starts making things happen.

Those are the STOPS – what are the STARTS?

Follow this program for creating Ultimate Customer Experiences:

START making great first impressions! And, if the impression has already been made on customers and colleagues you've been working with for a period of time, start by renewing and refreshing the impression they have of you with your new attitude and responsibility.

START getting it right! "Good enough" just isn't in today's competitive world! Don't settle for merely "OK" – get it EXACTLY right for your colleagues and customers!

START serving with empathy! When you show you truly care about how others feel, and that you are willing to take responsibility to do what you can to assist them, you create lifetime connections.

START connecting with emotion! The worst line I have ever heard someone say in a professional setting is, "Nothing personal – it's just business." Anyone who would make such a declaration knows zero about both. If we don't take our efforts for our organization personally, customers will take their business elsewhere!

And, START taking personal responsibility! The old cliché is: "If it is to be, it is up to me." Truer words were never spoken. Not only the customer's experience – but also your personal success and satisfaction – are the result of you taking responsibility.

It IS up to *you*!

UCE Checklist

1. Name a time when you were dissatisfied as a customer and someone took personal responsibility and assisted you.
    a. How did their efforts make you feel about the organization that had disappointed you?
        i. How did you feel about the person who took responsibility and helped solve your problem?
2. When have you made excuses about your personal performance?
    a. When was the last time you did it?
        i. What did you say?
3. What are the excuses you use most frequently?
    a. Write down a list!
        i. Take the personal responsibility to eliminate these excuses from your communications with customers!

Conclusion

There you have it! The five steps to create an Ultimate Customer Experience:

- Make a GREAT First Impression
- Don't Make It Right...GET It Right!
- Serve With Empathy
- Connect With Emotion
- Take Personal Responsibility

Your efforts are more important than ever before, because customer loyalty is changing! I would suggest there were formerly three distinct levels of customer loyalty.

Level One consisted of those customers only interested in transactions. They went for the cheapest, operating almost as if they were seeking bids for their business. The only loyalty they displayed was to price. Unfortunately, for many businesses -- and the professionals like you who work for them -- we tend to overestimate the percentage of customers and prospects at Level One. It makes sense for ALL customers to inquire about pricing...yet we often mistake a reasonable question for a price objection.

Level Three held those customers who, to use Ken Blanchard's terrific term, are "Raving Fans." They aren't merely customers; they are *advocates* of your products and services. They are passionate about the relationship they have with you -- and you may count them among your best friends in your personal life, as well as terrific customers. No business or professional can have too many listed at Level Three.

Between these are those at Level Two, who are -- to be quite imprecise -- "kind of" loyal. In other words, they have a high degree of connectivity to you...however, they also have a similar level of loyalty with some of your competitors. They have a smaller cadre of suppliers where they place their business, yet they are not the exclusive type of advocates found at Level Three. Obviously, it's always been vital to have many at Level Two as well, because they can deliver a significant degree of high quality business to you and your organization.

The problem -- in today's economy, as well as our contemporary culture -- is that Level Two is evaporating.

We're seeing customers either becoming more focused on the relationship with a trusted supplier...finding it more advantageous to tap into the expertise, quality, and Ultimate Customer Experiences delivered by a valued professional like you -- OR -- seeking the quickest, cheapest transaction possible.

What contributes to lack of loyalty? We only have to look at television -- and the declining loyalty to both networks and to individual programs -- to see the pattern. A terrific column by Dave Morgan, CEO of Simulmedia, on OnlineSpin from MediaPost.com, outlines the three major contributors to this phenomenon.

1) So many good choices. There are lots of great TV programs...and you have lots of worthy competitors. This sheer explosion of options means customers can be like "kids in a candy store" in just about any industry, including yours.

2) Poor information and navigation. For broadcasting, it means, "There are no tools available today that can easily inform viewers in a timely way about all of the available programming that they might enjoy." For your business and career, it might mean customers and prospects are under-informed...or misinformed...and, therefore, cannot make decisions that would break your way.

3) Changing loyalties. Morgan suggests for TV it means viewers are now loyal to "their TVs, to the days and times when they turn them on, and to favorite genres of programming. Most are no longer loyal to specific programs or networks." Today's technology also means that if you can't be home watching "Family Guy" on Sunday night…it's no problem. Where a few years ago it meant you would miss the program altogether, now you just record it and watch it at home when you desire — or go to Hulu.com and see it on your laptop.

Have you thoroughly examined how the shifts in technology and buyer behavior are changing not just the loyalty of customers…but, more importantly, HOW and WHAT they are loyal to?

It's simply common sense if we're seeing erosion at Level Two — and we don't want to compete on merely price — we have to learn and execute the strategies that will enhance engagement and multiply the number of customers we have at Level Three.

The most important aspect, it seems to me, is we must focus more than ever before on creating "Ultimate Customer Experiences." As mentioned earlier, *your* efforts are now **more important than ever!**

Make it a JOY!

Frankly, as I was working on this book, I originally had an additional step: "Make it a Joy!"

Ever notice someone who is really passionate about their work? In my small hometown of Crothersville, Indiana, the owner of our solitary funeral home is Mark Adams. Now, I realize "joy" may be an unconventional word to use in describing a funeral home director; however, having used his services for the funerals of my father and grandmother, I can attest he delivers that to his customers.

He's so passionate about his job – and making certain a sad situation is handled with the utmost compassion and integrity – it becomes a joy to be his customer.

However, as I was writing the chapter on the additional step, I suddenly realized to "Make It A Joy" isn't a step you take – instead, it is the *result* that occurs when you do the five steps we've already discussed!

Please don't misunderstand, I believe organizations -- and individuals like you -- should do everything in your power to make certain customers enjoy the process of doing business with you.

An article in Forbes magazine discussed that effort: "consumers who want fun as much as products are finding it in some unlikely places. Bank of America is the nation's largest consumer bank, but it doesn't want to act like one. That's why tellers at its 4,000 branches have recently started bolting their posts to hop around in conga lines. On 'Hawaiian Fridays' they open accounts and accept deposits in grass skirts. At Bank of America these antics are the result of mandatory 'spirit training,' developed because bank brass want employees to have the…demeanor of workers in Disney theme parks…(and) Bank of America insists customer satisfaction is soaring."

The effort to inject enjoyment into business interaction is a part of why I wrote my first book, "ALL Business is Show Business!"

However, there is something deeper and more important here.

YOU go FIRST…

The late author and broadcaster Earl Nightingale told the story that success is like a person and a wood stove. If you want heat, you have to put wood in the stove and set it ablaze. It would never occur to you to say to the stove, "If you first give me heat, *then* I will put in some wood."

Yet, Nightingale wisely observed, that is exactly how most people behave when it comes to their personal satisfaction and success. We seem to say, for example, "If customers were nicer to me, then I would treat them better!" Or, "No one else here cares for customers, why should I go first?"

In other words, we are saying, in essence, "Give me heat before I put in the fuel."

It doesn't work with stoves…your car won't give you transportation and let you put in the gasoline *after* you arrive at your destination…and it doesn't work in creating Ultimate Customer Experiences, either. YOU have to go FIRST!

But then, something amazing begins to happen – you begin to make it a joy for a customer to be engaged with you. It's the result of your actions in making the five steps a reality for your customers.

One of the greatest lessons in life is to realize that our lives mirror ourselves. In other words, the way people usually treat you is a reflection of how they perceive you are treating them. The level of success you have attained in your career is approximately equal to the relative effort and commitment you have invested into it.

When you execute these five steps, and become a joy for customers to work and deal with, their joy will reflect back to you – and your life and your job becomes infinitely more rewarding in ways you never previously imagined.

Here's the catch: YOU have to go FIRST.

Does it work every time? No, of course not – what does? Even a baseball player making $25 million a year only gets a hit about three out of every ten times at bat! Michael Jordan missed more shots than he made. Great chefs have made inedible dishes. No one, regardless of his or her level of expertise, knowledge, and ability, can make something work every single time.

The key is the phrase *"more often than not."* While another hitter might strike out in a pressure situation, *more often than not* the superstar will deliver. That's why he gets $25 million and the other batter, while still a terrific player, will earn much less. The chef may occasionally make a bad dish, but *more often than not,* you are going to want to dine at her restaurant.

You may have a favorite movie star – for me, it's Robert Duvall. Your favorite, like mine, has undoubtedly made some bad movies. However, *more often than not,* you know what he or she is going to be in is going to be spectacular. It's why they have become our favorites!

Delivering the Ultimate Customer Experience means **significantly** *more often than not,* customers are going to be thrilled to be doing business with you – and will share that joy with their friends (meaning you have more customers and your business does better)…and with you (meaning work and life becomes more rewarding).

It's the mirror effect: the joy you create for your customers – internal and external -- becomes the joy you enhance for yourself.

As I wrote those words, I can almost hear some readers saying, "Come on, you can't be serious! If you think work can be fun – even joyous – then you've never worked where I do!"

And, you're probably right about one aspect – I've almost certainly never worked where you do, as this book will go to literally thousands of companies.

However, I would ask you to consider this point: By saying what

I've just imagined – "work can't be fun or joyous where I work" – you are doing exactly what we discussed in the previous chapter about personal responsibility. It's not your company's mission to make your job enjoyable. It's your responsibility.

My Dad was a butcher who would go on farms in the middle of winter and work for farmers butchering their cattle. The conditions in the cold and with his job were worse than I could endure. Yet, my father loved it…because he chose to. His enthusiasm was contagious, and his customers reflected it back to him – making his work, to him, a joy.

(You can read more about how his work impacted many lives in my previous book, "Create Distinction: What to Do When 'Great' Isn't Good Enough to Grow Your Business.")

If you can find a way to make butchering cattle in snow and subzero temperatures joyous…it's hard for me to truly believe you cannot find a little more impact and meaning in your work.

But, it is your choice. You have to go first.

Thank you…

Your time and effort to read this book is something for which I am truly and profoundly grateful. And, I can assure you if you follow the five steps we have been discussing, your customers will be truly and profoundly grateful to YOU for creating an Ultimate Customer Experience for them!

Here's to an exciting, joyous future in your new career – as the Chief Executive Officer of creating Ultimate Customer Experiences for the people YOU encounter!

Scott McKain -- June 4, 2013

Scott McKain's Biography

Scott McKain is an internationally known expert who helps organizations create distinction in every phase of business and teaches how to deliver an "Ultimate Customer Experience®."

Scott McKain creates captivating presentations and bestselling books which clearly reveal how to create more compelling connections between you and your customers and how to stand out and move up, regardless of the economic climate in your industry.

Scott McKain's calling is business – and his passion is platform presentations. He is a unique combination of vast speaking experience and new, cutting-edge information. His presentations benefit from three decades of experience, combined with his innate talent for articulating successful ideas. McKain has spoken before and consulted for the world's most influential corporations.

In today's Facebook/Twitter/social media world, a dissatisfied customer now has a platform to broadcast his or her opinions regarding your organization to the world instantaneously. In this environment, it's never been more important to understand and execute the steps necessary to create the "ultimate customer experience." McKain is one of about 150 living members of the Professional Speakers Hall of Fame. He was also recently recognized by Social Media Marketing Magazine as one of the fifty most influential marketing authors on Twitter and GenJuice, a leading resource for emerging professionals, as one of the "Top 25" people for Gen Y and Millennial leaders to follow on Twitter.

There are a myriad of choices in the marketplace for prospects and customers seeking the products and services of your industry.

So, how does your organization – and the professionals who work with you – stand out from the plethora of competitors?

In his book, Create Distinction, (expanded and revised release of bestselling book, "Collapse of Distinction" — named by thirty major newspapers as one of the "Ten Best Business Books" of the year and reached the number one spot on Amazon.com's list of business bestsellers), McKain takes a revolutionary approach by showing how organizations and individual professionals create differentiation in the marketplace.

McKain has appeared multiple times as a commentator on FOX News to discuss business, politics, and American culture. In his earlier career as a broadcast journalist, two million people saw his commentaries each week on 80 television stations in the United States, Canada, and Australia. He has also been a news anchor for a CBS-TV affiliate in one of the nation's 25 largest markets.

McKain has been named as a "Hoosier Hero" in his home state because of his commitment to youth and philanthropy. He was selected by Arnold Schwarzenegger to be the emcee and speaker for the Great American Workout, held on the White House lawn with the President in the audience carried live on CNN and NBC's "Today" show. He also portrayed the villain in a film by internationally esteemed director Werner Herzog, acclaimed by critic Roger Ebert as one of the "best movies" ever made.

Bibliography

GradView.com; "How Not to Act in a Job Interview" -
http://www.gradview.com/articles/careers/big_mistake.html

AllBusiness.com; "The Importance of First Impressions" -
http://www.allbusiness.com/10590845-1.html; by Barry Himmel;
originally published in Rental Product News; February 2008

The Elsmar Cove Forum: Internal Customers -
http://elsmar.com/wiki/index.php/Internal_Customer (Elsmar
Cove Quality Assurance and Business Standards Wiki)

"The Fred Factor: How Passion in Your Work and Life Can Turn
the Ordinary into the Extraordinary"; Mark Sanborn; Broadway
Business; 1st edition; April, 2004

http://dictionary.reference.com/browse/empathy

Customer Service definitions:
http://www.financialcrisis2009.org/forum/Corporations/What-
would-be-the-perfect-definition-in-explaining-what-customer-
service-means-to-you-216020.htm

"Serving the customer: Main Street Conversation ... Rita Vogler."
Hesperia Star (Hesperia, CA). McClatchy-Tribune Information
Services. 2007. Retrieved May 24, 2010 from HighBeam
Research: http://www.highbeam.com/doc/1G1-159250887.html

Cassano, Erik. "Galplin Motors Inc.: Fast track." Smart Business
Los Angeles. Smart Business Network. 2007. Retrieved May 24,
2010 from HighBeam Research:
http://www.highbeam.com/doc/1P3-1288642111.html

"Undercover Boss Goes E-Commercial" CBS.com;
http://www.cbsnews.com/stories/2010/03/22/entertainment/main
6322460.shtml

"Why It Pays to Go the Extra Mile"; "From the Dean";
November 2004; https://www.bridgeport.edu/pages/3529.asp

"United Breaks Guitars: Did It Really Cost The Airline $180
Million?" Ryan McCarthy;
http://www.huffingtonpost.com/2009/07/24/united-breaks-
guitars-did_n_244357.html July 2009

"Revenge is best served cold – on YouTube: How a broken guitar
became a smash hit"; The Times; London; Chris Ayres; July
2009;
http://www.timesonline.co.uk/tol/comment/columnists/chris_ayre
s/article6722407.ece

"It Really is a Personality Contest." PR News. Access
Intelligence, LLC. 2006. Retrieved June 03, 2010 from
HighBeam Research: http://www.highbeam.com/doc/1G1-
141724095.html

"Measuring Up," CFO Magazine; June 26, 2007; quoted on
"Enterprise Engagement Alliance Networking Expo" homepage:
http://www.eeaexpo.com

"Loyalty Rules: How Today's Leaders Build Lasting
Relationships," Frederick F. Reichheld; Perseus; September 2001

"The Six Pillars of Character," Josephson Institute; quoted from:
http://josephsoninstitute.org/sixpillars.html

"The Sequence of Personal Responsibility"; Ron Haskins, Senior
Fellow, Economic Studies; The Brookings Institution;
Washington, DC; quoted from:
http://www.brookings.edu/articles/2009/0709_responsibility_has

kins.aspx

"Most TV Viewers Don't Know What to Watch"; Dave Morgan; MediaPost.com; quoted from:
http://www.mediapost.com/publications/?fa=Articles.showArticl e&art_aid=119335

"Funny Business"; Forbes Magazine; by Monte Burke; June 2003; quoted from:
http://www.forbes.com/forbes/2003/0609/173.html

Websites and Contact

Scott McKain's websites include:

http://ScottMcKain.com

http://McKainViewpoint.com (Scott's blog on business and the customer experience)

http://ProjectDistinct.com (Short ideas to stand out and move up)

http://CreateDistinction.com (on Scott's latest book)

You can follow Scott on Twitter -- @ScottMcKain

You can friend Scott on Facebook – https://www.facebook.com/pages/Scott-McKain-Speaker-Author/192569100779605?fref=ts

Watch Scott's videos on YouTube on the Scott McKain Channel: http://youtube.com/scottmckain

The Scott McKain Channel on Live365.com streams Scott's audio content twenty-four hours a day, seven days a week. Listen at: http://live365.com/stations/scottmckain

Scott has a channel on Blog Talk Radio where he hosts live talk shows, and you can download previous shows and podcasts: http://www.blogtalkradio.com/scottmckain

Scott is also on other social media sites such as LinkedIn and Google+ -- just do a search for him and join the conversation!

Scott McKain